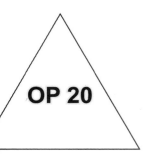

OP 20

Operation AL FAJR:
A Study in Army and Marine Corps Joint Operations

Matt M. Matthews

D1280715

Combat Studies Institute Press
Combined Arms Center
Fort Leavenworth, Kansas

Library of Congress Cataloging-in-Publication Data

Matthews, Matt M., 1959-
   Operation al-Fajr : a study in Army and Marine Corps joint operations / By
Matt M. Matthews.
   p. cm.
   Includes bibliographical references and index.
   1. Iraq War, 2003- . 2. Fallujah, Battle of, Fallājah, Iraq, 2004. 3. Combined
operations
   (Military science). 4. Unified operations (Military science). 5. United States--
Armed forces.
   I. Title.
   DS79.766.F3M38 2006
   956.7044'342--dc22

                                                                  2006028778

First Printing: October 2006
Second Printing: January 2008
Third Printing: March 2009

CSI Press publications cover a variety of military history topics. The views expressed in this CSI Press publication are those of the author and not necessarily those of the Department of the Army, or the Department of Defense.

A full list of CSI Press publications, many of them available for downloading, can be found at http://usacac.army.mil/CAC2/CSI/.

For sale by the Superintendent of Documents, U.S. Government Printing Office
Internet: bookstore.gpo.gov   Phone: toll free (866) 512-1800;   DC area (202) 512-1800
Fax: (202) 512-2250 Mail: Stop IDCC, Washington, DC 20402-0001

ISBN 0-16-076877-2

Foreword

The two battles for the Iraqi city of Fallujah in 2004 were turning points in Operation Iraqi Freedom. Elements of the US Marine Corps began an offensive in April to destroy enemy forces in the town, but the battle ended prematurely with the Marines being replaced by the "Fallujah Brigade," followed soon after by a complete enemy takeover of the city. Some units of the new Iraqi Army were also committed to the first battle; they were found wanting and the entire Iraqi training program significantly changed in response. In November 2004, a combined USMC, US Army, and Iraqi Army offensive succeeded in eliminating the enemy in Fallujah in a destructive urban battle. In Operation AL FAJR: A Study in Army and Marine Corps Joint Operations, Mr. Matt Matthews focuses on the ways in which Army and Marine forces operated together in the second Battle of Fallujah.

Among the many Army units that participated, Task Force 2-2 Infantry and Task Force 2-7 Cavalry spearheaded the attacks of two Marine regimental combat teams into and through the city. Matthews' gripping narrative describes their role in the battle from notification, to planning, and through the fighting to the conclusion of their role in the battle. With access to first-person accounts and unit histories from both task forces, Matthews' monograph illuminates many aspects of the battle which have been missing from popular journalistic accounts.

Army–Marine interoperability is the theme around which Matthews bases his account. Well-educated and professional Army and Marine leaders at the Lieutenant Colonel and Colonel levels overcame many ingrained cultural differences to synchronize operations. Army senior NCOs and junior officers displayed tremendous initiative, flexibility, and courage in fighting alongside their Marine counterparts. They skillfully exploited the incredible firepower, survivability and urban mobility of Army heavy forces to destroy enemy resistance in some of the most brutal urban combat of the war. Matthews also addresses areas in which the Army and Marines must continue to improve their ability to fight side by side.

Operation AL FAJR is a compelling case study of combat at the tactical level in Operation IRAQI FREEDOM. Army–Marine relations have improved greatly since the acrimony that sometimes plagued the WWII era. As Matthews makes clear, there is more work to be done. *CSI—The Past is Prologue!*

Timothy R. Reese
Colonel, Armor
Director, Combat Studies Institute

Acknowledgments

This Global War on Terrorism paper could not have been written without the help of many veterans of Operation PHANTOM FURY/AL FAJR. In countless hours of interviews, they shared moments of military triumph and personal loss. Many times, those interviewed contacted other veterans who in turn telephoned or e-mailed me, eager to offer their personal accounts as well. They welcomed the opportunity to tell their stories and were grateful the Combat Studies Institute (CSI) wanted to document their experiences. I am indebted to them for their candor and the trust they have placed in me to write their story.

CSI's Operational Leadership Experience (OLE) team was also instrumental in bringing this paper to fruition. Under the leadership of Mr. John McCool, the OLE team was able to transcribe and archive each interview related to the second battle of Fallujah. I would like to thank team members Dr. Christopher K. Ives for his interviews and the transcribing work done by Ms. Jennifer Vedder and Ms. Colette Kiszka.

I want to thank Mr. Kendall D. Gott, Senior Historian, Research and Publications Team for his advice on this project and CSI historian Mr. John McGrath for his guidance and assistance with the Fallujah maps. I appreciate the assistance of my office mate and fellow historian, Dr. Tom Bruscino, as well as the efforts of our editors, Ms. Angi Bowman, Mrs. Catherine Small, and Ms. Jennifer Lindsey, each of whom played a role in the completion of this project.

I would like to acknowledge Colonel Timothy R. Reese, Director, CSI; Dr. William G. Robertson, Deputy Director, CSI and CAC Command Historian; and Lieutenant Colonel Steven E. Clay, former Chief, Research and Publications Team for their advice and support in this effort.

Finally, a special thanks to my wife, Susan Day Harmison, for her support and encouragement throughout this process.

Contents

Introduction

Joint operations are here to stay. Everybody's lived it and watched it work. We could not have fought this fight without the joint piece.

Lieutenant General (LTG) John F. Sattler, US Marines

In November 2004, the 1st Marine Division (1 MAR DIV) stormed into Fallujah, Iraq, launching an all-out effort to destroy insurgents and foreign fighters within the city. Initially designated Operation PHANTOM FURY, the name was changed at the last minute to Operation AL FAJR (New Dawn) to more adequately reflect Iraqi partnership in the endeavor. Long before this bloody engagement ended, the second battle of Fallujah claimed its place in the pantheon of illustrious Marine Corps battles. LTG John F. Sattler, Commander of the 1st Marine Expeditionary Force (I MEF) predicted, "The heroics and tactical details of the battle of Fallujah will be the subject of many articles and books in the years to come."[1]

The vast majority of the American public, however, does not know the decisive and gallant role of the US Army in this operation.[2] The Army's 2d Brigade Combat Team, or "Blackjack Brigade" from the 1st Cavalry Division (2BCT/1CD) was instrumental in sealing off Fallujah from the south and east. At the same time, two US Army heavy-mechanized battalions, Task Force (TF) 2-7 and TF 2-2 stood at the forefront of 1 MAR DIV's assault into the city. It could be convincingly argued their bold and decisive actions did much to facilitate the ultimate victory.

The Army and Marines have, at times, experienced an ambivalent working relationship. Since World War I, acrimony and egos have occasionally flared, marring the alliance between the two fighting forces and complicating battlefield cohesion. Would the joint effort of Operation AL FAJR result in continuing discord, or would this unified mission allay such rivalries?

According to Sattler, "Operation AL FAJR was joint and coalition warfare at its finest."[3] Major General (MG) (Retired) John Batiste, who commanded the 1st Infantry Division (1ID) and provided forces for the battle from his own 3d Brigade Combat Team, (3BCT\1ID) stated there

1

was "great teamwork" between the Army and Marines and no problems existed between the two services.[4] Colonel (COL) Michael Formica, commander of the "Blackjack Brigade," called the operation "Unbelievable." He concluded that he "could not have been more proud of the soldiers and marines that executed these tasks. We task organized Army and Marine forces down to platoon level. I had Marine squads operating inside of infantry platoons . . . I had tank and Bradley platoons and sections task organized to Marine reconnaissance companies . . . It all worked very well."[5] Major (MAJ) Sean Tracy, a joint fires and effects planner in III Corps, thought "the fight . . . set the standard. You can probably write the book on joint operations from this operation."[6] Bing West, author of *No True Glory: A Frontline Account of the Battle of Fallujah*, is certain that in Fallujah "the operational cooperation between the two services reached a new zenith."[7]

This Global War on Terrorism (GWOT) Occasional Paper will focus on the tactical and cultural interactions between the US Army and US Marine Corps units which assaulted into Fallujah, specifically the US Army TF 2-7 and TF 2-2, and the US Marine Corps Regimental Combat Team-1 (RCT), and RCT-7.

Is it possible, after years of discord and interservice jealousy, that a new era in joint interdependence and collaboration between the Army and Marines was born? Relying almost exclusively on interviews with Operation AL FAJR participants, this paper will attempt to answer this important question.

Chapter 1 deals briefly with the long-standing rivalry between the Army and Marines and examines the origin of the discord. It also addresses the first Marine assault on Fallujah, Operation VALIANT RESOLVE, and the Battle of Najaf. Both of these operations were instrumental in the Marines identifying the need for Army heavy- mechanized forces. Chapter 2 addresses the planning and integration of TF 2-7 and TF 2-2 into RCT-1 and RCT-7 prior to the execution of Operation AL FAJR. Chapter 3 discusses the joint assault on Fallujah and examines the complexities of the joint operation. The final chapter offers an analysis of the cohesive nature of the effort and lessons learned from the endeavor.

Undoubtedly, the Army and Marines will continue to work together in the Global War on Terrorism. It is hoped this work will prove beneficial for Marine and Army officers who find themselves involved in future joint operations. This paper demonstrates that exemplary leadership relies on cooperation and mutual respect, and that difficulties inherent in a shared mission can be overcome.

Notes

1.   Lieutenant General John F. Sattler and Lieutenant Colonel Daniel H. Wilson, "Operation AL FAJR: The Battle of Fallujah-Part II," *Marine Corps Gazette,* (July 2005), 24.

2.   "Imagine my surprise," wrote renowned journalist Bill Kurtis, "when I learned that the Army actually led the attack on Fallujah." Bill Kurtis, e-mail interview by author, 25 April 2006.

3.   Sattler and Wilson, Operation AL FAJR, 16.

4.   Major General (RET) John Batiste, e-mail interview by author, 14 April 2006.

5.   Colonel Michael Formica, telephone interview by author, 21 April 2006.

6.   Major Sean Tracy, interview by author, Fort Leavenworth, Kansas, 15 March 2006.

7.   Bing West, *No True Glory: A Frontline Account of the Battle for Fallujah,* (New York: Bantam Books, 2005), 355.

Chapter 1

Interservice Rivalries, Operation VALIANT RESOLVE and the Road to the Joint Assault on Fallujah

Casualties many; Percentage of dead not known;
Combat efficiency: we are winning.

COL David M. Shoup
US Marines, Tarawa, 1943

And then we'll have to take a little jaunt against the purple-pissing
Japanese and clean their nest too, before the Marines
get in and claim all the goddamn credit!

General (GEN) George S. Patton

The Marine Corps has just been called by the New York Times
'The elite of this country.' I think it is the elite of the world.

Admiral (ADM) William Halsey

For your information, the Marine Corps is the Navy's police force
and as long as I am President that is what it will remain. They
have a propaganda machine that is almost equal to Stalin's.

President Harry S. Truman

Interservice Rivalries

While the American military emerged victorious in World War I, the conflict spawned a bitter enmity between the US Army and US Marine Corps. Although the Marine Corps represented only a small fraction of the American troops fighting in France during World War I, they managed to capture a large portion of the headlines. While certainly valiant and courageous, they were no more heroic than the Army units they fought beside. Aggressive Marine Corps recruiting tactics, combined with sensational press accounts, created an atmosphere of hero worship in which Marines were seen as nearly single-handedly vanquishing enemies. While their efforts were indeed meritorious, they were not without equal.[1]

GEN John J. Pershing, commander of the American Expeditionary Force (AEF), was so disconcerted by the publicity showered on the Marines, he refused to accept a new Marine brigade or create a Marine division to serve in France. By the close of the war, the acrimony between the Army and Marines was fully apparent. Many Army officers, who later rose to key leadership positions in World War II, viewed the Marine Corps with suspicion. According to historian Allan R. Millett, World War I proved costly to Army and Marine relations. "The principle loss was the chance for harmony with the United States Army, for some of the Army's senior officers returned from the war convinced that the Marine Corps would do anything it could to belittle the regular Army's reputation."[2] Apparently, the war also left Harry S. Truman, a young US Army field artillery captain, with bitter feelings toward the Marines.

With America's entry into World War II, the festering legacy of Army and Marine animosity continued. On Corregidor in 1942, for example, GEN Douglas MacArthur refused to endorse a presidential unit citation for the 4th Marines, arguing "the Marines had enough glory in World War I."[3]

The biggest controversy of the war erupted on Saipan in 1944, when Marine MG Holland M. "Howling Mad" Smith relieved Army MG Ralph C. Smith of command. Holland Smith accused Ralph Smith, commander of the 27th Infantry Division, of a lack of leadership and lack of aggressiveness. Soon, Army LTG Robert C. Richardson, Jr., entered the fray, accusing the Marines of an inability to control units above division level. The ensuing firestorm caught the attention of the press, with one news organization accusing the Marines of unimaginative tactics that "led to heavy casualties," while other national periodicals stood solidly with the Marines.[4] Although both Smiths were shuffled off to new assignments, Army and Marine relations remained strained. GEN George C. Marshall was apparently so incensed by the incident he "vowed that he would never permit another soldier to serve under a Marine command."[5]

After World War II, President Harry S. Truman was convinced the military should present a more unified, cohesive fighting force. In 1946, he ordered the Joint Chiefs of Staff (JCS) to review the situation and offer viable strategies. It came as no surprise when the JCS, which held no Marine representatives, recommended a diminutive Marine Corps with no units above the size of a regiment. Understandably, the Marines were incensed by the proposal. It was only through the efforts of the lobbying arm of the Chowder Society[6] that the proposed legislation was defeated in Congress.

Marine Corps lobbying efforts proved so successful that the National Security Act of 1947 provided an expanded role for the Marines. The Act specifically allowed the Marines to have "fleet marine forces of combined arms, together with supporting air components, for service with the fleet in the seizure or defense of advanced naval bases, and for the conduct of such land operations as may be essential to the prosecution of a naval campaign."[7] While the Marines were jubilant, the Army was extremely disappointed with the Act. GEN Dwight D. Eisenhower was particularly outraged, convinced that the Marines were "so unsure of their value to their country that they insisted on writing into law a complete set of rules and specifications for their future operations and duties. Such freezing of detail . . . is silly, even vicious."[8]

With America's entry into the Korean War in the summer of 1950, Marine Corps promoters increased pressure on Congress for further expansion of their force. Responding to a congressman about the impending legislation, President Truman wrote that "Nobody desires to belittle the efforts of the Marine Corps, but when the Marine Corps goes into the Army, it works with and for the Army and that is the way it should be." When the letter was made public, this remark, along with several other disparaging comments about the Marines, caused a national uproar.[9]

As the fight to expand the Marine Corps continued in Congress, GEN Omar N. Bradley accused the Marines of a conspiracy. One of his aides told the press that the General was certain the Marines were determined to become America's "second" Army. According to Millett, Bradley also "argued that press reports from Korea unfairly condemned the Army's performance and glorified the 1st Marine Division."[10] By the close of the Korean War, the acrimony between the Army and Marines was still palpable.

The hostilities between the Army and Marines continued during the Vietnam War. GEN William C. Westmoreland reportedly advised his superiors that he "distrusted Marine operations."[11] Westmoreland's replacement, GEN Creighton Abrams, was even more venomous in his assessment of the Marine Corps. When pressed to accept a Marine general as his deputy, Abrams responded:

> What I prefer to address are the professional qualifications of any
> Marine to be Deputy Commander, US Military Assistance Command

Vietnam (COMUSMACV). In my judgment no Marine has the full professional military qualifications to satisfactorily discharge the military responsibilities of the office . . . While the Marines are second to none in bravery, esprit and the intrinsic quality of their men, I consider them less professionally qualified in the techniques and tactics of fighting than the U.S. Army, the Korean Army and the Australians. The Marines have in the main been slow to adapt innovations, tactics, techniques and devices which would make their forces more effective against a frequently cunning and clever enemy. They have not been imaginative in developing ways to optimize their strong points against the enemy weak points. Their inertia is to keep on with the pedestrian tactics they thought were right in the beginning. The Marines believe implicitly in giving a man a job and letting him do it. I am satisfied that will not work here . . . It is not enough to die for your country. If that is your sacrifice then in the case of the combat man it should be made exacting the greatest price from the enemy . . . This is a hard, tough war, demanding the best in professionalism. It cannot be prosecuted with mirrors, words or tradition.[12]

Fortunately for the nation, the Army and Marines began making significant strides in restoring goodwill between the two services in the mid-1980s. With the passing of the Goldwater-Nichols Department of Defense Reorganization Act of 1986, the former rivals began a gradual shift away from old parochialisms and interservice rivalries. This act and the Department of Defense organizational changes that followed pushed all the services toward joint operations, and according to Marine LTG John F. Sattler, caused a "cross-pollination" of the various branches. Sattler was certain that, "What began in 1986 with the sweeping organizational changes wrought by the Goldwater-Nichols Act had brought invaluable returns for US service members in modern-day combat operations." Sattler was also convinced that the Army and Marine school system played a major role in bringing the two services back into a more harmonious relationship. "Sitting next to each other in professional schools over the years, those relationships come into play."[13]

Sattler was correct. In both the 1991 Gulf War and Operation IRAQI FREEDOM in 2003, the Army and Marines reached new levels of cooperation. However, as author and former Assistant Secretary of Defense Bing West points out, " . . . while the two Gulf Wars (1991 and 2003) erased mutual suspicions between the two services and proved the soundness of joint planning at high levels, each service fought as a separate entity at the division level." A closer, albeit potentially more volatile coupling would not occur until Operation IRAQI FREEDOM II in 2004, when both Army and Marine battalion-size elements were placed under the tactical control (TACON) of each service.

Operation VALIANT RESOLVE and the Battle of Najaf

Operation VALIANT RESOLVE, the first Marine assault on Fallujah, began on 5 April 2004 in response to the killing of four American contractors in the city. Ordered to apprehend the assailants, two Marine battalions began a series of deliberate attacks against insurgent positions.

Confronted by approximately 300,000 civilians and 2,000 insurgents, the Marines were hard pressed from the beginning. Although they successfully cordoned off the city, the Marines simply lacked the strength to defeat the insurgents. In his article, "Who Won the Battle of Fallujah," which appeared in the US Naval Institute's *Proceedings*, Jonathan F. Keiler states that, "In some important respects, the initial push into Fallujah violated guidelines in the Corps' urban warfare manual, Marine Corps Warfighting Publication (MCWP) 3-35.3." Keiler maintained:

> . . . the objectives and means of Valiant Resolve became incompatible. Two reinforced battalions were tasked with isolating and attacking a medium-sized city . . . Depending on the tactical situation, manpower shortages may be compensated for by increased firepower, which the Marine commanders were unwilling-or unable-to apply in Valiant Resolve. Indeed, it appears that leaders at the scene quickly came to this conclusion. The operation never progressed beyond the foothold stage. Marines gained access to the urban area (in that case, outlying industrial neighborhoods), but did not penetrate to the heart of the city, much less take it.[14]

In his book *Fiasco,* Thomas E. Ricks wrote that "the enemy was better prepared than the Marines had been told to expect." A Marine summary of the operation noted, "insurgents surprise U.S. with coordination of their attacks: coordinated, combined, volley-fire RPGs," and "effective use of indirect fire. Enemy maneuvered effectively and stood and fought."[15]

While the rules of engagement (ROE) for Operation VALIANT RESOLVE were restrictive and limited the application of Marine Corps firepower (air and indirect fire), the Marines possessed limited heavy-armor assets, which curtailed their ability to deliver overwhelming direct-fire support. Casualties may well have been fewer with the use of more tanks and other heavily armored vehicles. In his article "Lack of Heavy Armor Constrains Urban Operations in Iraq," David Wood claimed, "The Marines . . . are using only 16 tanks in Iraq of their inventory of 403, and have deployed 39 of their 1,057 assault amphibian vehicles that provide protection against small arms but not rocket-propelled grenades."[16]

Although the Marines ordered two additional infantry battalions into Falluajh, it was to no avail. After suffering heavy losses and decisively losing the Information Operations (IO) campaign, the Marines pulled out of Fallujah the first week in May. While some would argue the battle was lost solely in the IO arena, Keiler believed the assignment was "beyond their [the Marines] capabilities, at least within what was deemed to be acceptable limits of friendly and civilian casualties and property destruction."[17]

The Marines turned security of the city over to the pro-government "Fallujah Brigade," which by summer's end either deserted or joined the insurgents in Fallujah. The insurgents and foreign fighters in the city considered the Marine withdrawal a great victory and in many respects served to embolden the insurgency, not only in Fallujah, but throughout Iraq. By mid-summer 2004, Fallujah was totally controlled by insurgents and foreign fighters who organized and launched attacks not only against the Marines outside the city, but throughout the country.

In August, while I MEF kept a watchful eye on Fallujah, the city of Najaf exploded, as Muqtada al Sadr's anti-government Mahdi militia attacked government forces in the city. The 11th Marine Expeditionary Unit (MEU) received orders to stop al Sadr's militia and restore order in Najaf. Not long into the fight, 11th MEU called for reinforcements. LTG Thomas F. Metz, Commander of US Army III Corps and Multinational Corps-Iraq (MNC-I), quickly ordered in heavy-mechanized forces from the 1st Cavalry Division. On 7 August, US Army TF 1-5 arrived in Najaf, followed on 10 August by TF 2-7 that was positioned outside the city.[18]

For the next three weeks, the 11th MEU, TF 1-5 and TF 2-7, along with pro-government Iraqi forces, pounded al Sadr's Militia. Marine and Army forces killed approximately 1,500 of al Sadr's men while American casualties were comparatively light.[19] With the success in Najaf, all eyes turned back toward Fallujah. MNC-I ordered I MEF to begin planning for a new assault on the insurgent stronghold of Fallujah on 10 September.[20] For this second round, the Marines were determined to bring US Army tanks and Bradleys into the fray.

Notes

1.   MAJ James P. O'Donnell, "The Struggle For Survival," GlobalSecurity.org, http://www.globalsecurity.org/military/library/report/1985/OJP.htm (1985), 4.

2   Allan R. Millett, Semper Fidelis: The History of the United States Marine Corps The Revised and Expanded Edition (New York: The Free Press, 1980), 307, 317-318.

3.   William Manchester, American Caesar: Douglas MacArthur 1880-1964 (Boston: Little, Brown and Company, 1978), 230.

4.   Forrest C. Pogue, George C. Marshall: Organizer of Victory (New York: The Viking Press, 1973), 448.

5.   Ibid, 450; By far the best comprehensive history of the Smith versus Smith controversy can be found in Harry A. Gailey, Howlin' Mad VS The Army: Conflict in Command, Saipan 1944 (Navato: Presidio Press, 1986).

6.   The Chowder Society was a Marine lobbying organization consisting of 12 Marine officers. O'Donnell, "The Struggle for Survival."

7.   O'Donnell, 8.

8.   Ibid, quoted in Robert H. Ferrel, The Eisenhower Diaries (New York: W.W. Norton and Co, 1981), 142.

9.   Letter, Harry S. Truman to Congressman Gordon L. McDonough, 29 August 1950, Truman Library, "Public papers of the Presidents: Harry S. Truman," http://trumanlibrary.org/publicpapers/viewpapers.php?pid=864

10.   Millett, 497-498.

11.   Bing West, No True Glory: A Frontline Account of the Battle for Fallujah (New York: Bantam Books, 2005), 354.

12.   Lewis Sorley, Thunderbolt: General Creighton Abrams And The Army Of His Times (New York: Simon & Schuster, 1992), 209.

13.   Gina Cavallaro, "Old Parochialisms' of U.S. Services Have Yielded to 'Cross-Pollination,' Battlefield Commander Says," Defense News Media Group Conferences Joint Warfare 2005, http://www.defensenews.com/promos/conferences/jw/1204577.html

14.   Jonathan F. Keiler, "Who Won the Battle of Fallujah?" U.S. Naval Institute Proceedings, January 2005.

15.   Thomas E. Ricks, Fiasco: The American Military Adventure in Iraq (New York: The Penguin Press, 2006), 333.

16.   David Wood, "Lack of Heavy Armor Constrains Urban Options in Iraq," Newhouse News Service, 27 April 2004. http://www.newhousenews.com/archive/wood042704.html

17.   Keiler.

18.   John R. Ballard, Fighting For Fallujah: A New Dawn for Iraq (Westport: Praeger Security International, 2006), 29-37.

19.   bid, 36.

20.   Ibid, 44.

Chapter 2

Planning and Integration for Operation Phantom Fury

Guys talk about Military Operations on Urban Terrain (MOUT) being the right place for light infantry, but very few understood the power of a mechanized heavy battalion in an urban environment.

Lieutenant Colonel (LTC) Pete Newell
Commander Task Force 2-2, US Army

With the prevalent Low Intensity Conflict (LIC) mentality inundating the Corps, there has developed a mind set that small and light is good, and big and heavy is bad. The truth be told, small and light equates to weak and dead.

Major (MAJ) Dennis W. Beal, US Marines, 1991

Early into the deliberate planning for Operation PHANTOM FURY, 1st Marine Division (1 MAR DIV) Commander MG Richard F. Natonski and his staff recognized the need for US Army heavy-mechanized forces. "Starting in September 2004," Natonski recalled, "we identified the requirement for additional forces."[1] Natonski's Regimental Combat Team-1 (RCT-1) Commander, COL Michael Shupp, was more succinct, recollecting that, "during this planning phase, we saw that we needed more combat power to thwart the enemy and their defenses. We didn't have enough heavy armor to go in there with us, nor were there enough Iraqi forces with us."[2]

Natonski made an immediate request for additional support to the commander of the I Marine Expeditionary Force (I MEF), LTG John F. Sattler. Sattler then ran the additional support request up to his superiors, US Army Commander of Multinational Forces-Iraq (MNF-I), GEN George Casey and US Army III Corps and Multinational Corps-Iraq (MNC-I), Commanding Officer LTG Tom Metz. One recent account suggests Sattler called Metz directly and requested the 2d Battalion, 7th Cavalry Regiment (TF 2-7), 2d Battalion, 2d Infantry Regiment (TF 2-2), and the "Blackjack Brigade" (2d Brigade Combat Team, 1st Cavalry Division [2BCT/1CD]).[3]

Natonski describes a less dramatic, albeit far more accurate picture of Sattler's request, stating that Sattler knew better than to ask for specific units. "Sattler went to Casey and Metz with our requirements for additional forces," Natonski remembered. "He asked for capabilities, for example 'mech armor' for the assault into the city and then went on to mention 2-7 CAV and 2-2 INF . . . I know those were the two units he wanted but he was astute enough not to blatantly ask for them by name, only mentioning that they were good units and we had worked with them before."[4]

Task Force 2-2 Integration into RCT-7

By the first week in October, 1ID was ordered by MNC-I to provide a heavy-mechanized task force to 1 MAR DIV's Regimental Combat Team-7 (RCT-7). Batiste gave the mission to his 3d Brigade Combat Team (3BCT/1ID) operating out of the Diyala Province.[5] COL Dana Pittard, commander of 3BCT/1ID, tasked LTC Pete Newell's TF 2-2 whose battalion was stationed at Forward Operating Base (FOB) Normandy near Muqdadiyah, approximately 75 miles northeast of Baghdad. Newell recalled this was initially a mission no one thought would come to fruition. "It was one of those cases where you said, 'Yeah, right.'"

Despite early uncertainty, the mission would actually take place. Newell, along with his company commanders, operations officer, (S3) MAJ John Reynolds, the battalion intelligence officer (S2), and the 3BCT operations officer, MAJ Ken Adgie, flew west to Al Asad to link up with RCT-7 Commander COL Craig Tucker and his staff.

"In early October, we were given the warning order that said it may possibly happen, and we actually conducted a visual [reconnaissance] with 7th Regimental Combat Team Headquarters out in Al Anbar Province sometime that month," Newell said.

It was during this recon that Newell and Reynolds informed Tucker and his staff the TF 2-2 force package would include three companies and noted they would also need assets not organic to the task force. Reynolds recalled requesting a list of resources from the Marines including Raven unmanned aerial vehicles (UAV), a military intelligence analyst cell, ammunition (Class V), medical material (Class VIII), repair parts (Class IX), a liaison officer (LNO) for RCT-7, a tactical satellite (TACSAT), a AN/TTC-48 (V) small extension node switch (SEN), and engineer support.

Newell outlined the capabilities a heavy-mechanized task force would bring to the table in the upcoming fight for the Marine command staff.

MAJOR GENERAL NATONSKI BRIEFS TASK FORCE 2-2 COMPANY
COMMANDERS PRIOR TO THE ASSAULT ON FALLUJAH.

From the collection of Lieutenant Colonel John Reynolds

Newell was convinced that "very few understood the power of a mechanized heavy battalion in an urban environment."[6]

At this time, the Marine commander's intent was to employ TF 2-2 as a blocking force south of the city and as a security force protecting the main supply routes (MSR) into Fallujah. RCT-7 also produced a wide-ranging list of "be prepared to" (BPT) missions. These BPTs included securing the industrial area of Fallujah, an attack into the northeastern part of the city, as well as securing Phase Line (PL) FRAN also known as Highway 10.[7]

Showing remarkable flexibility, RCT-7 planned to attach a Marine light armored vehicle (LAV) company to TF 2-2. According to Reynolds, "this indicated that early in RCT-7's planning cycle they were integrating our capabilities and theirs to achieve a desired end state."[8] Indeed, from the very beginning, Sattler and his Marines were determined to overcome interservice rivalries and parochialisms and RCT-7 proved from the onset they were fully committed to a successful joint operation. Sattler stated that, "No one came up and said, 'This isn't how we do it.' Everybody got what they needed across the board."[9]

By the end of the meeting, TF 2-2 had a good understanding of the intent of the operation. The task force staff left the meeting with the Marines believing they had been included as equal participants in planning for the upcoming battle. According to Reynolds, "the entire staff was present . . . welcomed us and made us feel as part of the team."[10]

Looking back on the planning process, Jane Arraf, correspondent for CNN and a keen observer of events surrounding the planning and execution of the operation, attributed the successful integration of TF 2-2 into RCT-7 to the rapport established early on between Tucker and Newell. The two men were "incredibly smart so they got along and were on the same page," Arraf explained. "There is a huge cultural difference between the Marines and the Army, but I think what bridged it, in this instance, in Fallujah, was the skill of the commanders, because you could tell they were on the same page."[11]

Despite the cohesive team being built between the Army and the Marines, neither Newell nor Tucker knew exactly how TF 2-2 would be task organized for the upcoming operation. More importantly, no one knew for certain when the attack on Fallujah would begin.[12]

After returning from Al Asad, Reynolds learned that instead of the three companies they planned taking with them to Fallujah, 3BCT/1ID had reduced their complement to elements of two companies: A Company, 2d Battalion, 2d Infantry Regiment (A/2-2) and A Company, 2d Battalion, 63d Armor Regiment (A/2-63).[13] Newell points out that the Fallujah operation was just a few short weeks before the scheduled elections and everyone's attention was focused on ensuring adequate security for that. It is possible this became a limiting factor in supporting operations in Anbar Province. When initially tasked, 1ID told MNC-I they could only provide two heavy company teams. However, "based on our recon and my discussions with COL Pittard, I know 3BCT wanted to give us three companies, but had to go to 1ID to get permission to add the third," said Newell.[14]

Once the change in available forces came down, Reynolds immediately made contact with RCT-7's staff to inform them because he knew that losing one company could greatly affect the overall mission. He also recognized the need to ensure the ROE for both the Army and the Marine units were identical and requested to see the Marine ROE. "I understood that we would fight as a joint force," Reynolds recalled, "and I wanted to ensure we swapped SOPs (standard operating procedures) and reporting procedures."[15]

Word came down to TF 2-2 on 8 October that the assault on Fallujah would not begin until after the Muslim holy days of Ramadan on 17 and 18 November. While its task organization for battle remained clouded and the exact time of the operation remained in limbo, the task force staff went to work developing its mission analysis and possible courses of action (COA).

During this time, the assistant S2 for TF 2-2, CPT Natalie Friel, received daily intelligence summaries (INTSUMs) from the Marines.[16] According to Friel, "They were always willing to drop all that they were doing (and they were extremely busy!) to walk me through the current intelligence situation and burn CDs with new imagery and UAV findings for me."[17]

On 17 October, LTC Robert Heidenreich, future operations and plans officer for RCT-7, informed Reynolds he was very impressed with TF 2-2's well-delineated control measures for Fallujah. According to Reynolds, "he liked our Fallujah numbering system where we added graphic control features to assist in controlling the fight. LTC Heidenreich said he would look at building one for the fight; eventually this turned into a joint product and the Air Force published a grid box system for the entire Fallujah area of operations which helped everyone see the battle and control the fight."[18] Undoubtedly, the successful planning and resulting implementation of the operation was due, in no small measure, to the willingness of the Marines to work in concert with all branches of the military service.

On 19 October, TF 2-2 learned from 1ID planners that Iraqi Prime Minister Ayad Allawi was considering launching the attack on Fallujah before Ramadan. 1ID planner, MAJ Kevin Jacobi, informed Reynolds that once Allawi made his decision, MNC-I would have at least 10 days to prepare for the operation. Significantly, TF 2-2 was informed that the "Blackjack Brigade" would be placed under the operational control of 1 MAR DIV and assigned the blocking and MSR security mission originally assigned to TF 2-2.[19]

With TF 2-2 no longer committed to a blocking and security mission, RCT-7 quickly incorporated them into a new course of action. TF 2-2 would now attack with RCT-7 into Fallujah. In the new plan, RCT-7, as the supporting effort for 1 MAR DIV, would attack into the city from north to south with three battalions abreast. The 1st Battalion, 8th Marines (1/8) would assault into the city on RCT-7's western boundary with 1st Battalion, 3d Marines (1/3) to its east. TF 2-2 would launch its attack into eastern Fallujah as the supporting effort for RCT-7. TF 2-2's mission was to pierce the enemy's defenses and rapidly secure Highway 10 or PL FRAN, as it was identified on 1 MAR DIV's control features.

"As we looked at the plan and talked about the things we could do," Newell recalled, "they [RCT-7] were very concerned about their MSR, the one that went from west to east in Fallujah [Highway 10] . . . That was the only way they were going to be able to resupply the units once they were in the city . . . [This is] what drove them to give us the eastern portion of the city with the role of getting to and opening Fran early on."[20] The RCT-7 plan also called for TF 2-2 to secure the industrial area of Fallujah and to conduct "search and attack" operations toward the southwest.[21] TF 2-2's planners went to work, quickly preparing the plan for this new mission.

On 22 October, TF 2-2 received the mission's task organization from COL Pittard. TF 2-2 would consist of A/2-2, A/2-63, and F Troop 4th Cavalry Regiment, (F/4CAV) as the brigade reconnaissance team (BRT), and HHC (-) with the task force's mortars and scouts. As Reynolds pointed out, each of the three units task organized to TF 2-2 were coming from three different locations in the 3BCT AO. This made it clear to Operation PHANTOM FURY planners that the 3BCT commander saw the need to maintain presence and combat power throughout his area of responsibility, despite the operations taking place in the west.[22]

"At this point we were reworking our data for our movement requirements to ensure our time line would not cause friction. What was interesting, however, was that all three companies were coming from three different locations within the brigade's area of operations, and the first time the entire team would be together was going to be Fallujah," Reynolds said.[23]

Reynolds and his planning staff also learned that an Iraqi Intervention Force (2/IIF) battalion (-) would be attached to the task force for the fight in Fallujah. "This was truly going to be a plug and play event. All companies and organizations would linkup at Fallujah just days prior to the fight; this meant that synchronization had to be done via e-mail and at meetings we had with the commanders at our recons in Fallujah," he remarked.

Fallujah Fragmentary Order (FRAGO) 221840 from 1 MAR DIV set the timeline for TF 2-2. The 1 MAR DIV FRAGO "identified us as being task organized (TACON) effective D-4 to RCT-7," Reynolds said. "Our combat power at this point was 14 M1s and 16 M2s. Our movement timeline was D-5 for the advance party and D-4 for the main body."[24]

On 23 October, Reynolds and the company commanders conducted a ground reconnaissance to Camp Fallujah. As RCT-7 rolled into Camp Fallujah from Al Asad, they spoke with Tucker about the upcoming operation. At this meeting, Tucker reaffirmed TF 2-2 would indeed receive the two companies comprising 2d Battalion, Iraqi Intervention Force (2/IIF), to assist in the assault on Fallujah. Three days later, on 26 October, RCT-7 issued a draft FRAGO which, according to Reynolds, "was very precise," and "provided excellent coordinating instructions, and allowed us to continue our planning."[25]

By most accounts, 29 October was a crucial day in TF 2-2's integration into RCT-7. On this day, Pittard and Reynolds met with Tucker at Camp Fallujah. This wasn't the first meeting between Pittard and Tucker. Both men were what military insiders call "Jedi Knights," graduates of the

Army's School of Advanced Military Studies (SAMS). The shared experience provided the two commanders with a common operating concept of doctrine and strategy.[26]

During the meeting between Pittard and Tucker, Pittard agreed to provide TF 2-2 with engineer and artillery assets. The support would include a mine clearing line charge (MCLIC) and two M109A6s (155mm Paladin's), additional assets Newell had already identified as mission essential for the fight. Both TF 2-2 and RCT-7 would come to rely heavily on this equipment in the fight that was to come.

Reynolds believed "the significance of this meeting would facilitate not only our rapid success but also the success of RCT-7 . . . We needed breaching assets to breach the railroad berm . . . we needed fire support under our direct control because TF 2-2 would not receive any from 1 Mar Div; we were not the main effort, in fact we were the supporting battalion effort to RCT-7's supporting effort . . . "[27]

This meeting provided one more opportunity for the commanders and planners to examine a map of Fallujah and discuss tactics, terrain, obstacles, and strategy. "Over a large map," Adgie recalled, "Colonel Tucker and the rest of us talked about what the scheme of maneuver would look like; we exchanged viewpoints and things like that."[28]

As discussion of the Fallujah mission continued, TF 2-2 recognized the need for a liaison team to be on station in the RCT-7 tactical operations center (TOC). Reynolds assigned First Lieutenant (1LT) Jeff Jager and 1LT Christopher Lacour and several officers to serve as liaison officers to RCT-7. Initially, Jager and the LNO team experienced some frustrations with the lack of compatibility between Marine and Army communications system. Because of the inhospitable operating environment at Camp Fallujah, Marine communication capabilities were not as robust as they would have been had the environment been less austere. Because of the secure nature of the information the LNO team had to pass back to TF 2-2 headquarters, they needed access to secure computer lines, and though the team had adequate hardware, they didn't have compatible access to the secure lines.

"We had four secure internet protocol router (SIPR) computers between members of the LNO team, and all of us had our own, but RCT-7 was operating pretty austerely. They weren't at their home base camp; they

TASK ORGANIZATION TF 2-2

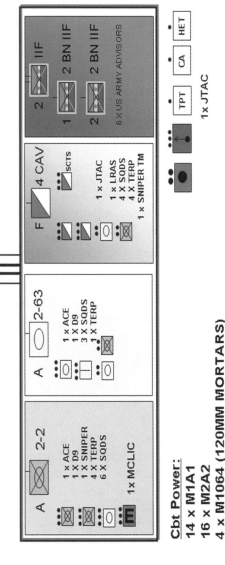

A 2-2
- 1 x ACE
- 1 x D9
- 1 x SNIPER
- 4 x TERP
- 6 x SQDS

1 x MCLIC

A 2-63
- 1 x ACE
- 1 x D9
- 3 x SQDS
- 1 x TERP

F 4 CAV
SCTS
- 1 x JTAC
- 1 x LRAS
- 4 x SQDS
- 4 x TERP
- 1 x SNIPER TM

2 IIF
- 1   2 BN IIF
- 2   2 BN IIF

6 X US ARMY ADVISORS

TPT   CA   HET

1 x JTAC

Cbt Power:
14 x M1A1
16 x M2A2
4 x M1064 (120MM MORTARS)
2 x 81MM MORTARS
38 x M1114
16 x M998AOA
2 x M109A6 (155MM PALADIN)
1 x MCLIC (2 X RELOADS)
1 X GBS (PREDATOR (UAV DOWNLINK)
2 X RVT
1 X FORWARD EYES (SCAN EAGLE DOWNLINK)
3 X RAVENS

From the collection of Lieutenant Colonel John Reynolds

21

just had their organic commo equipment so they were very limited in the number of drops [secure Internet lines] they could give us," Jager said. "It wasn't like we could just take our computer, unplug it from our SIPR drop, plug it into the Marine Corps SIPR drop and have it work."

The problem with secure computer lines was eventually resolved by the RCT-7 communications officer (S6), but lack of computer lines were the least of the challenges the LNO team faced in the RCT-7 TOC.

> We also had the same problems with telephones. Initially, we couldn't dial an Army number from the Marine Corps phone at all. It took a couple of days but, eventually, the RCT-7 signal guys were able to figure out how to let us call back to FOB Normandy, but they could only give us one line that they could configure that way. They had to use all the others to talk to their chain of command. So the number we got, we established as the 2-2 TOC. But to call anybody else, like brigade or any other Army phone number, we had to go back through Germany, to a switchboard in Germany, to have them patch us into the Army network, which limited our ability but at least we were still able to communicate.[29]

Jager also observed how the Marines communicated and conducted command and control. "I was able to figure out that they used chat to communicate from battalion to RCT. I don't know what they used for battalion command and control, but their primary means of communication at the RCT level was SIPR chat. I understood that in the TOC by way of interaction with their watch officers and the battle staff. That's how they conducted operations."[30]

Lacour, who was also the assistant Fire Support Officer (FSO) for TF 2-2, explained the camaraderie he enjoyed in working with the Marines. "They were really great to work with and it was great to experience that. We met the RCT-7 Commander, Colonel Craig Tucker, and he was absolutely fantastic as far as planning and tactical competence and running meetings."[31] From a fire support perspective, Lacour found combining Marine and Army fire support to be a straightforward proposition. "Integrating with the fire support assets," Lacour recalled, "was pretty easy because the joint training the Marines and the Army go through makes it a lot easier . . . we all speak the same language, at least as far as cannon artillery goes."[32]

As the major combat elements of TF 2-2 prepared to move to Camp Fallujah and linkup with RCT-7, Newell, Reynolds, and the TF 2-2 company commanders took part in 1 MAR DIV's rock drill and maneuver rehearsal on 3 November. Perceptions of the effectiveness of the rehearsal varied among the Army company commanders in attendance. CPT Kirk Mayfield, Commander of F/4CAV BRT, recalled that although the Marines "used some different terms and acronyms, it was fine."[33]

On the other hand, CPT Paul Fowler, A/2-63 said that he experienced some problems with the "language barrier" between the Marines and the Army. "The Marines/Navy used some of the same tactical and strategic terminology that we did. However, it meant different things to them than to us."

"The biggest thing that . . . was disappointing," Fowler remembered, "was the plan was very disjointed and somewhat ambiguous." The company commander was quick to point out however, that "with the TF rehearsal, which included the IIF and RCT-7 representatives, the [company commanders and team leaders] got to talk/walk through their plans and contingency plans which was very helpful because we used all of them."[34]

Despite the differing perceptions of some involved in the rehearsal, Newell was ultimately convinced RCT-7 and 1 MAR DIV did an exceptional job in planning for Operation PHANTOM FURY. "I give [RCT-7] and the [1 MAR DIV] commanders an A+ in leadership, which is where integration starts," Newell said.[35] Newell, a veteran of many operations, stressed that in his opinion the Marines' planning process equaled that of the Army's. "The [RCT-7's] tactical planning was as good as any Army brigade I had been assigned to and in some cases surpassed that of my parent brigade. Most importantly was their willingness to listen and make changes based on our recommendations for our employment . . . I had no issues with their rock drills or rehearsals."[36]

By 5 November, TF 2-2 had fully assembled all of its assets at Camp Fallujah. On 7 November, RCT-7 issued its final order. The line of departure (LD) time for TF 2-2 was set. The task force would move out on D+1, 8 November 2004 at 1900.

Task Force 2-7 Integration into RCT-1

"We started getting rumblings," recounted MAJ Tim Karcher, operations officer for TF 2-7, "that we would be asked to come back to fight with the Marines around about early October." Karcher, also a graduate of SAMS, had been with TF 2-7 since July 2004. The battalion had already

From the collection of LieutenantColonel John Reynolds

LTC PETE NEWELL'S FINAL SPEECH TO HIS SOLDIERS PRIOR TO THE ASSAULT.

fought alongside the Marines in Najaf in August, where, according to Karcher, "We did some pretty robust destruction for them." In that battle, he felt his unit had little time to plan before being committed to the fight. He was determined that would not happen again.

Karcher and the Battalion Executive Officer, MAJ Scott Jackson, were concerned the brigade headquarters, the 39th Enhanced Brigade, Arkansas National Guard, was not providing timely information regarding possible deployment to Fallujah, and contacted planners at the 1st Cavalry Division for information. By mid-October, their doggedness prevailed and direct liaison with the Marines was authorized. In no time, Karcher was on his way to his first planning conference with COL Shupp's RCT-1. "We got in at the grassroots of their planning, were able to shape their course of action a little bit, their concept, to something that was more in line with our capabilities," Karcher explained.[37] Shupp was extremely impressed with Karcher when the young S3 arrived at Camp Fallujah to begin integration into RCT-1. Shupp noted his capabilities as a "great officer" who had been in combat or planning combat missions his whole time in theater.[38]

While Karcher believed TF 2-7 did not have enough time to plan prior to committing forces in Najaf, the battle nonetheless convinced the Marines of the exceptional fighting caliber of TF 2-7. According to CPT Michael S. Erwin, Assistant S2 for TF 2-7 during the battle of Najaf, "We got there at 0300 and started going to work right away trying to figure out what they wanted us to do. Right off the bat, we had a pretty close relationship working with them, especially Major Karcher. He came down there as the voice for Lieutenant Colonel James Rainey, our battalion commander, saying we would do whatever they needed us to do, and I think that really played a big role in it." Erwin continued, "There was no showing up and expecting a certain mission or a certain role. We just showed up there and knew we were there to help them. We knew they had a tough fight going on, so we were there to support them however we could. This helped with the Marines' perception of us as fighters; and once they gave us one of the tougher missions down there, it gave us the experience and we could prove we could continue to work for them and continue to support their mission."[39]

According to CPT Edward Twaddell III, Commander of A Company TF 2-7 (A/2-7), "One of the lessons that came out of Najaf was the requirement for good tie-in once the warning orders had been given at the battalion, brigade, regimental level . . . So my assumption is that folks took the lessons learned from Najaf and applied them and did a lot of good cross talk before we even left Taji to link in with them."[40] Without doubt, the fighting in Najaf had solidified TF 2-7's elite reputation within I MEF, which significantly assisted its smooth integration into RCT-1.

Early in November, Rainey and his TF 2-7 received the official warning order tasking them to initiate planning for operations in Fallujah. "We received a warning order from 1st CAV, and everybody kind of knew something was going down in Fallujah," Rainey explained "The Marines had asked for more forces and we got the warning order probably about 3 November. We found out we were going to be working with the Marines' 1st Regimental Combat Team, got linked up, and got them started in the planning process."[41]

A few days later, in the middle of the night, TF 2-7 along with the "Blackjack Brigade" (who controlled the move) rolled out of Taji heading for Camp Fallujah. Rainey and his task force would linkup with RCT-1 mission planners and Karcher, who had been forward with RCT-1 for several days. "We closed on Camp Fallujah initially, got into the process of planning with 1st RCT, conducting reconnaissance and getting our logistics footprint set. We had a great move; it's not a simple matter to move and deploy in the middle of the night. Second Brigade Combat Team (BCT) had a good plan, it was well supported, and then they chopped us over to 1st RCT."[42]

The soldiers' reception that first night at Camp Fallujah would set the tone for how the Marines and the Army worked together throughout the operation. For the most part, the soldiers of TF 2-7 said they were received positively. Command Sergeant Major (CSM) Timothy L. Mace, TF 2-7 was impressed by the Marines' willingness to immediately integrate the TF 2-7 troops into Camp Fallujah. "The Marines were extremely professional and I was very impressed with 1st Marine Regiment, 1st Marine Division," he recalled. "The regimental command sergeant major welcomed me right off the bat. 'Whatever your soldiers need, Camp Fallujah is open to you. If you ain't got it, you let me know and you'll get it.' " Mace stressed that, from the beginning, it was obvious throughout the Marine chain of command that this was a joint operation. "The Marine officers and staff officers, from the commander on down, [were] just excellent to work with. No difference between the Marines and the Army as far as having common purpose, common direction . . ." Mace said, looking back on that first night at Camp Fallujah.[43]

CPT Coley D. Tyler, FSO for TF 2-7, said that this operation changed his perceptions about working with the Marines. Coley recalled that he went into the mission in Fallujah believing many of the stereotypes about Marines that have developed from the oftentimes strained relationship between soldiers and Marines and the competitive rivalry of the two services. "However, I found the Marines were extremely intelligent, have a lot of common sense, and I actually enjoyed the way they ran their operation, almost more so than the Army," said Tyler.[44]

"From my point of view," said CPT Chris Brooke, TF 2-7 C Company Commander, "it was adequate. We rolled into Camp Fallujah and it was a pretty established base. They had a place for us to park our Bradleys . . . but the one thing that does stick out in my head is that there were no tents for my company. It wasn't a huge deal and we managed, but other than that it was fine."[45] It would appear the offer made to CSM Mace of ". . . if you ain't got it, you let me know and you'll get it" was a bit inflated.[46]

By the time Rainey arrived at Camp Fallujah, Karcher, who had been at Camp Fallujah for several days conducting mission planning, had already informed him of RCT-1's preliminary planning. Rainey recalled:

> The initial plan he [Karcher] got from 1st RCT was a very narrow penetration into the city along one axis of advance. When I got my first brief on the plan from our guys, I liked the fact that they had a pretty good intel situation-unlike Najaf, where we had no idea where the enemy was or what he was doing or how many civilians were there. The Marines had done a very solid intelligence preparation of the battlefield (IPB). They knew where the mosques were, they knew how many civilians were in the city, they had pretty good numbers on the enemy, they'd done a lot of analysis and they had really good maps, overhead imagery and such, so I felt really good about that. I liked the fact that 2-7 was going to be the main effort for 1st RCT, who was the main effort for the Marine Division (MARDIV)-so obviously I liked that for a lot of reasons. I knew their doctrine was the same as ours in terms of a main effort, and I knew we'd be resourced in terms of fires and collection assets as we needed to be. What I didn't like was the very narrow, limited mission . . . [Karcher] had been working with their S3 guys and he kind of explained that that might not be the optimal use of a mech battalion . . . Initially, my concern was that we needed more frontage, the ability to get more of our firepower into the fight than we could on one main route.[47]

Shupp knew that 1 MAR DIV was pushing for a single-axis penetration by TF 2-7 down route Henry, a major north-south road in RCT-1's eastern sector. He also knew Rainey and his staff were apprehensive about the limited nature of the proposed mission. MAJ Karcher explained:

> We actually told them, from experiences in Najaf, that they weren't going to bust a hole in his [the enemy] defenses because he's more mobile than you are and he doesn't have a command structure. He can just run to where the sounds of guns are. So we went back and forth on that and we essentially attacked on a broader front than they wanted to initially. Initially, they wanted us to make a couple block-wide penetration, but that made less sense than attacking across a broad front and killing as much as we could, to make it easier for the Marines to walk down to that decisive terrain, because that's how they got there.[48]

Karcher's thinking would prove prophetic. Shupp and his staff were indeed anxious to quickly capture the Jolan Park, a crucial piece of terrain in RCT-1's sector, which had been identified by Marine intelligence as a possible assembly area for insurgents.[49] Rainey explained the intricate machinations of the planning process between TF 2-7 and RCT-1:

> I asked Colonel Shupp for some more battle space and explained to him that Route Henry was an axis of advance that would let us get maybe two tanks into the fight at one time. We had 14 tanks and 30 Bradley's and I really felt like we could do more for the RCT if we had more battle space. So I looked west for more space because the east was a very limited option . . . that part of the city had the older Byzantine type architecture, the streets don't make sense, etc. He told me he did not want to buy off more battle space. He liked the fact that he was the main effort. He was concentrated on one quarter of the city, 7th RCT had the other three, and he didn't want to go that way. Obviously, he was the commander and so that was fair. The initial mission had 3d Battalion, 1st Marine Regiment (3-1) attacking the Jolan Park, which was the geographical center of gravity of the area 1st RCT had. It was the only open area and was the logical rallying point. There was a Ferris wheel, you could see it pretty well from a distance, and 1st RCT's intel assessment was that the enemy would use that as a rallying point. So 1st RCT thought the enemy would fight all over the city and then fall back to Jolan Park as a final defense; and the MARDIV's plan was to directly attack that with 1st RCT as the main effort and give the other three quarters of the city to 7th RCT. As we're looking at this-Tim Karcher, Mike Erwin, Captain Dave Gray, the intel guys, and my fires guy-we came up with an option that would take Alpha 2-7 and attack as the 2-7 main effort, do a frontal assault, direct attack on about three different roads, with a platoon on each road. We thought we could seize the Jolan Park with Alpha 2-7, acknowledging that we weren't going to go building to building. We'd kill anybody we saw that presented themselves,

within the rules of engagement (ROE), but we were not going to clear towards the Jolan Park; we were just going to attack it and then seize it. At the same time, we could put [C/3-8] on Henry and still get everything in the fight that we would anyway-because we could only get a couple tanks up front-and use them as a supporting effort to Alpha 2-7. So we would move them on parallel and [C/3-8] secures the flank, still conduct the penetration and still kill anybody that wants to fight. We offered that up to 1st RCT and Colonel Shupp said that if we could do that, it would be great, so that's the plan we settled on. Alpha 2-7 as the main effort, frontal assault, north to south, with two tasks: destroy enemy forces and seize the Jolan Park. That was supposed to take about a day. 3-1 would follow Alpha 2-7 and do the detailed clearance to complete the destruction of the enemy. They would use the Jolan Park to do a passage of lines through us and then turn west down to the river, while 3d Battalion, 5th Marine Regiment (3-5) secured the initial foothold in the corner and also had a detailed clearance: a complete-the-destruction type mission. It wasn't a negotiation. Colonel Shupp denied my first request and granted my second request. He listened to feedback and made a decision, just like good commanders do. The fact that he was receptive to listening and acknowledged the fact that we probably were the experts on how to employ mechanized assets impressed me very much.[50]

Mace was also impressed with both his officers and the Marines. "I will tell you there were no three finer officers in the entire theater for this fight than Lieutenant Colonel Rainey, Major Scott Jackson, and Major Tim Karcher. All these guys are Jedi Knights, meaning graduates of SAMS, and they were actually making sure that what people were doing was doctrinally correct and was resourced accordingly."

Mace went on to say, "We were just impressed to hear these guys. A little terminology back and forth: 'the Marines want us to do this, but what we should be doing is . . .' that sort of thing. Whenever our guys had input like that, it was well received. The Marines said, 'This is what we want you to do. Army: execute.' "[51]

Interestingly, Shupp was also a SAMS graduate and had attended the US Army Advanced Armor course and Cavalry Leaders course. From their first meeting, Shupp, Rainey, and Karcher developed a solid relationship. Rainey was instantly impressed with Shupp's ability to incorporate his mechanized capabilities into the fight. Rainey also appreciated Shupp's willingness to listen to the tankers, who were the subject matter experts on the use of tanks in an urban fight. "I finally met Colonel Shupp: Great guy, all about team building, and he went out of his way to make sure we had everything we needed . . . I was very impressed. He's obviously a very competent, successful infantryman, a warrior spirit kind of guy and very aggressive. He was really looking forward to finishing the fight in Fallujah."[52]

Rainey's impressions were mirrored by Shupp's impression of the 2-7 leaders. "The whole time, Karcher and 2-7 are working like they had been with us all the time," Shupp explained. "I can't stress enough . . . these guys were incredible . . . everything from their language to their morale to their attitude, just fit in perfectly with the Marine regiment. They were complete professionals, and I think a lot of that was established by Jim Rainey when he came down. Very aggressive, very good officers, knew their craft, and were prepared to go into combat and do the right thing."[53]

Task Force 2-7's LD time was set for the early evening of 8 November. The plan called for Marines from 3-1 to create a breach on the west side of the Fallujah train station allowing TF 2-7, (RCT-1's main effort), to launch its assault into the city. From there, TF 2-7 would attack to destroy the enemy forces in the Jolan District and prevent the enemy from using the Jolan Park as an assembly area.[54]

Formica's "Blackjack Brigade" had also been well integrated into the 1 MAR DIV's plan and was prepared to guard the movement of the assault battalions into their attack positions, interdict insurgents, and isolate Fallujah from the south and southeast. Demonstrating, once again, its commitment to a joint operation, 1 MAR DIV assigned a Marine reconnaissance battalion to "Blackjack." "To my great pleasure," Formica mused, "there wasn't a lot of difference. We spoke task and purpose. We all worked hard to understand the capabilities of the organizations, and our communications equipment [was] all compatible, so it was a good news story . . . The key takeaway for me was the manner in which they executed air/ground operations and deconflicted fires and close air support."[55]

Brigadier General (BG) Richard P. Formica, former Joint Fires and Effects Coordinator, MNC-I, agreed with COL Formica's assessment, affirming that the Marines were "absolutely brilliant in planning the operational/tactical fight in Fallujah across the spectrum of operations: civil-military operations (CMO), information operations (IO), lethal effects, and tactical ops."[56]

Task Organization TF 2-7

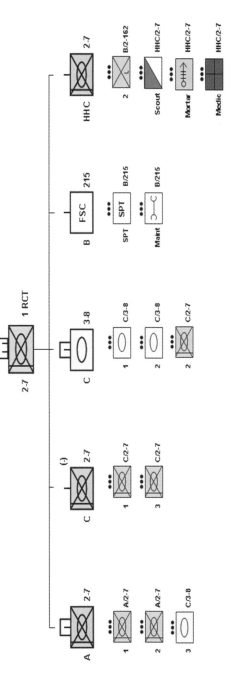

14/30/12/12
M1A2 SEP/M2A3/UAH/Rifle Squads

Courtesy of Task Force 2-7

The 1st Marine Division's preparation phase of the operation was over by 6 November. Natonski and his staff had successfully completed operational planning, the movement of forces, and the integration and training of Iraqi security forces. Most importantly, RCT-1 and RCT-7 had effectively integrated TF 2-7 and TF 2-2 into their operations, setting the conditions for success.

Perhaps the tribulations incurred in the April Battle of Fallujah made it clear to the Marines that a joint operation would be needed for a successful assault on the city. Sattler underscored the need for unity, noting "We could not have fought this fight without the joint piece."[57]

The success of the planning was due in large part to the willingness of the commanders and their staffs to share and receive input in an open and amenable manner. Many involved in formulating the operation had learned from the same doctrine and approached the joint mission with a sense of professionalism and respect for their counterparts. The Marines proved willing to listen to the counsel of the Army commanders and staffs. Army leaders seemed also willing to accept a subordinate position to 1 MAR DIV. By any criteria, the successful integration of US Army forces into 1 MAR DIV was an impressive accomplishment. The greatest challenge, however, was yet to come as Marine and Army forces crossed the LD into the city of Fallujah and the assault began.

TASK ORGANIZATION

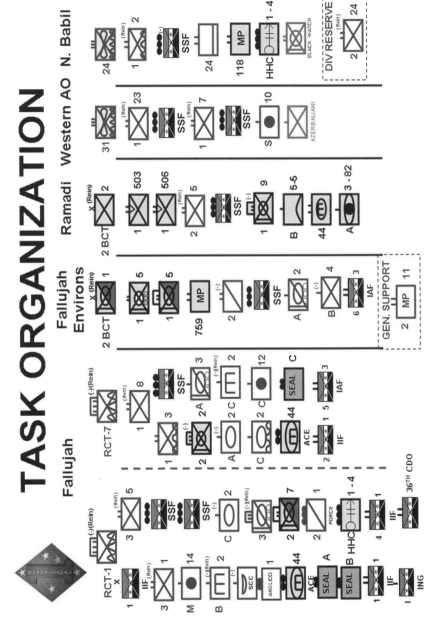

Credited to 1st Marine Division Commander Major General Richard F. Natonski

33

Notes

1.   MG Richard F. Natonski, e-mail interview by author, 8 March 2006.

2.   COL Michael Shupp, telephone interview by author, 25 March 2006.

3.   Bing West, No True Glory: A Frontline Account of the Battle for Fallujah (New York: Bantam Books, 2005), 259. While certainly colorful, West's work is also limited and parochial.

4.   MG Richard F. Natonski, e-mail interview by author, 8 March 2006; LTC Pete Newell thought "this discussion took place much later in October or early November after TF 2-2 had already been identified by 1ID as the unit that would fill I MEF's requirement. "I would characterize it," Newell stated, "as more of a formal request (for forces that had previously been tasked) made in the final days prior to the attack when I MEF was directed to assemble the assault force." LTC Newell, e-mail interview by author, 31 May 2006.

5.   Ibid.

6.   LTC Newell, telephone interview by author, 23 March 2006.

7.   LTC John Reynolds, interview by author at Fort Leavenworth, Kansas, 14 March 2006.

8.   Ibid.

9.   Gina Cavallaro, "Old Parochialisms of U.S. Services Have Yielded to Cross-Pollination, Battlefield Commander Says," Defense News Media Group Conferences, http://www.defensenews.com/promos/conferences/jw/1204577. html. (accessed 1 March 2006.)

10.   Reynolds interview.

11.   Jane Arraf, telephone interview by author, 3 April 2006.

12.   Reynolds interview.

13.   Newell pointed out that "at the time A2/2 was task organized with two organic M2A2 equipped platoons and an engineer platoon 2/A/82EN. A/2-2's other M2A2 platoon was attached to F/4 CAV at FOB Warhorse, given the limitations of just two teams and no combat support we were going to have to strip out the engineer platoon and add a tank platoon from B/1-63AR (we eventually got permission to take both platoons) and A Company, 2d Battalion 63d Armor Regiment A/2-63 (with two M1A1 tank platoons and a HMMWV mounted tank platoon." Newell, e-mail interview by author, 31 May 2006.

14.   Ibid.

15.   Reynolds interview.

16.   Ibid.

17.   CPT Natalie Friel, e-mail interview by author, 10 March 2006.

18.   Reynolds interview.

19.   Ibid.

20.   Newell interview.

21.   Reynolds interview.

22. Ibid.

23. Ibid

24. Ibid.

25. Ibid.

26. LTC Ken Adgie, interviewed by author Fort Leavenworth, Kansas, 8 March 2006.

27. Reynolds interview

28. Adgie interview.

29. CPT Jeff Jager, telephone interview by author, 17 May 2006.

30. Ibid.

31. CPT Christopher Lacour, telephone interview by author, 15 May 2006.

32. Ibid.

33. CPT Kirk Mayfield, e-mail interview by author, 9 March 2006.

34. CPT Paul Fowler, e-mail interview by author, 4 April 2006.

35. Newell interview.

36. Ibid.

37. MAJ Tim Karcher, telephone interview by author, 14 March 2006.

38. Shupp interview.

39. CPT Michael S. Erwin, telephone interview by author, 19 April 2006.

40. CPT Edward Twaddell III, telephone interview by author, 28 February 2006.

41. LTC James Rainey, telephone interview by author, 19 April 2006.

42. Ibid.

43. CSM Timothy L. Mace, telephone interview by author, 19 April 2006.

44. CPT Coley D. Tyler, telephone interview by author, 20 April 2006.

45. CPT Chris Brooke, telephone interview by author, 1 May 2006.

46. Mace interview.

47. Ibid.

48. Karcher interview.

49. Shupp interview.

50. Rainey interview.

51. Mace interview.

52. Rainey interview.

53. Shupp interview.

54. "TF 2-7 CAV Joint Operations in Fallujah, November 2004 Lessons Learned Packet" produced by TF 2-7 staff.

55. COL Michael Formica, telephone interview by author, 21 April 2006.

56. BG Richard P. Formica, interview by Patrecia Slayden Hollis, editor, "Part II: Joint Effects for the MNC-1 in OIF II," Field Artillery: A Joint Magazine for US Field Artillerymen, (August 2005), 11.

57. Cavallaro.

Chapter 3

The Joint Assault on Fallujah

*It's a man-on-man fight, a classic infantry battle . . . If you've got
a guy sitting in a house with two grenades, who knows he is going to die, were going to root these guys out, house by house.*

COL Craig Tucker, Commander
Regimental Combat Team-7, US Marines

*'Keep hammering targets and if you see a guy with an AK-
47, I expect you to hose him with a .50 caliber machine-gun.'
If firing was identified from a house, then artillery fire should
be called in to 'pancake the building because there is not a
building in this city worth one of our soldiers' lives.'*

LTC Pete Newell, Commander
Task Force 2-2, US Army

With six months to plan, enemy forces in Fallujah had established
well-prepared defensive positions. American forces entering the city would
face a bewildering array of improvised explosive devices (IEDs), vehicle-
borne improvised explosive devices (VBIEDs), mines, roadblocks, strong
points, and well-constructed fighting positions. Many of the insurgents
were foreign Islamic extremists who were more than willing to die. Convinced they had stopped the Marines in April, the insurgents appeared con-
fident of victory.

The First Marine Division's major combat components consisted of
RCT-1 and RCT-7, which would sweep into the city from the north. In
the west, TF 2-7 would lead the way for RCT-1, while TF 2-2 attacked
south through the eastern side of the city with two Marine battalions from
RCT-7. By 7 November, 1 MAR DIV, employing leaflet drops, loudspeak-
ers, and handbills, persuaded most of the civilian population to leave the
city. Natonski's division also conducted a series of feints, raids, and cor-
don searches, which confused the insurgents, and according to Natonski,
caused a "heightened state of paranoia and anxiety." More importantly,
the Marines initiated indirect fires and close air support (CAS) onto sus-
pected IEDs, VBIEDs, and enemy fighting positions. On 7 November, the
"Blackjack Brigade" shifted into its blocking position south and southeast

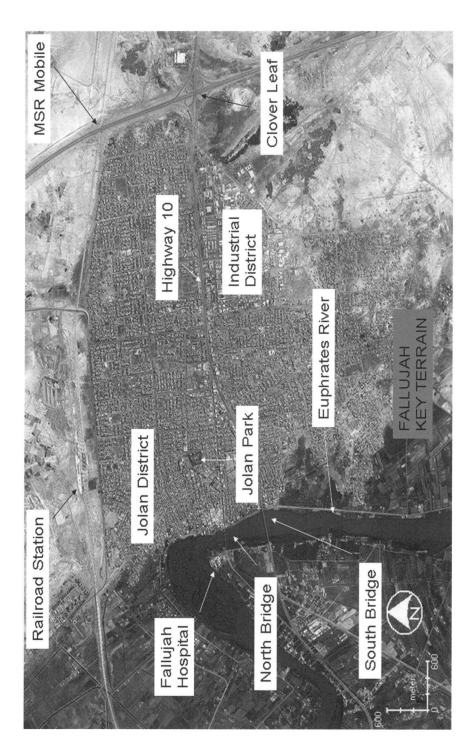

FALLUJAH
KEY TERRAIN

MSR Mobile

Clover Leaf

Highway 10

Industrial
District

Euphrates River

Railroad Station

Jolan District

Jolan Park

Fallujah
Hospital

North Bridge

South Bridge

N

600
meters
0
600

of the city, while the assault forces moved into their attack positions north of the city. In the west, 1 MAR DIV captured the Fallujah hospital and secured the bridges over the Euphrates River. The city was now completely sealed off from the outside world and for the next 24 hours, joint fires continued to wreak havoc on enemy positions.

RCT-7/TF 2-2 Joint Assault into Fallujah

On the morning of 8 November, CPT Kirk Mayfield and his BRT moved rapidly from attack positions northeast of Fallujah into their support-by-fire (SBF) positions on the northeastern edge of the city. Using both direct and indirect fires, Mayfield's men managed to kill over 35 insurgents and knock out several enemy strong points over the course of the day.[1]

CPT Paul Fowler's A/2-63 rolled out of the attack site at 1714 and prepared to cross the LD to assume its attack-by-fire (ABF) position on the northern outskirts of the city. At that precise moment, a Raven UAV from TF 2-2 crashed to the ground. Twenty-four minutes later another TF 2-2 Raven plummeted from the sky. While the TF 2-2 operational summary of Operation PHANTOM FURY blames 1/3 Marines for a frequency conflict, MAJ Reynolds, the task force operations officer, stated, "We didn't know . . . It could have been the Marines . . . But it was definitely a radio frequency (RF) deconfliction [sic] that did not occur."[2] The assistant operations officer for TF-2-2, 1LT Jeff Jager, thought Air Force or Marine Corps and Navy Prowlers might have been the culprit, while the NCOIC for the UAVs concurred with Jager, relating that the "Marines had been jamming a number of frequencies that night."[3] Completely focused on its breaching operation, TF 2-2 had little time to consider the Raven mishap.

At 1900, Fowler's company crossed the LD and moved immediately into its ABF positions to provide covering fire for the breaching operation. Calling artillery and smoke onto the buildings to his front, Fowler ordered his tanks and Bradleys to fire three simultaneous volleys into the rapidly crumbling structures. "The results were exactly as we had hoped," Fowler recalled, "creating massive casualties and chaos within the enemy ranks, disrupting their ability to defend against the breach . . ."[4]

At 1915, the engineer assets attached to CPT Sean P. Sims' A/2-2 fired its MCLIC at the previously identified breach site. The initial detonation produced numerous secondary explosions caused by IEDs that insurgents had placed around the city. "When the big boom hit," MAJ (Dr.) Lisa

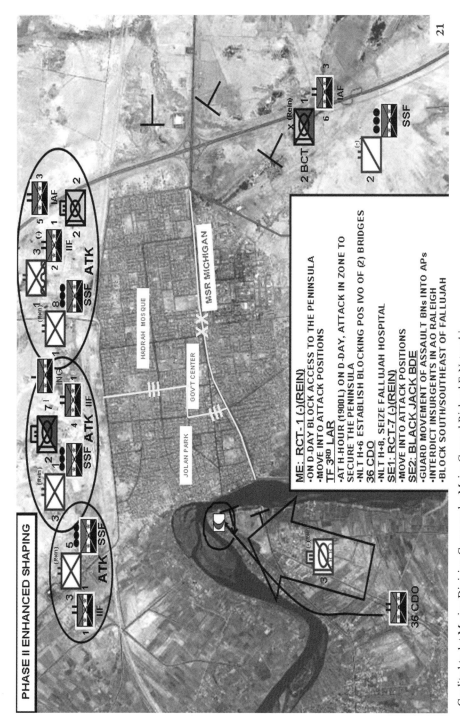

Credited to 1st Marine Division Commander Major Genreal Richard F. Natonski

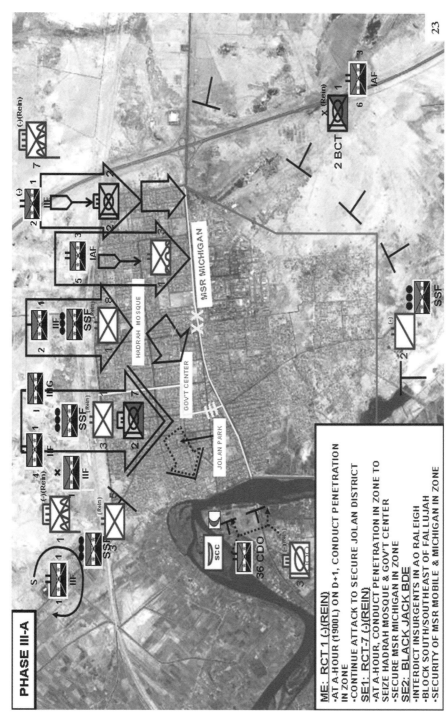

PHASE III-A

MSR MICHIGAN

HADRAH MOSQUE

GOVT CENTER

JOLAN PARK

SCC

36 CDO

2 BCT

IAF

SSF

ME: RCT 1 (-)(REIN)
- AT A-HOUR (1900L) ON D+1, CONDUCT PENETRATION IN ZONE
- CONTINUE ATTACK TO SECURE JOLAN DISTRICT

SE1: RCT-7 (-)(REIN)
- AT A-HOUR, CONDUCT PENETRATION IN ZONE TO SEIZE HADRAH MOSQUE & GOV'T CENTER
- SECURE MSR MICHIGAN IN ZONE

SE2: BLACK JACK BDE
- INTERDICT INSURGENTS IN AO RALEIGH
- BLOCK SOUTH/SOUTHEAST OF FALLUJAH
- SECURITY OF MSR MOBILE & MICHIGAN IN ZONE

Credited to 1st Marine Division Commander Major General Richard F. Natonski

23

41

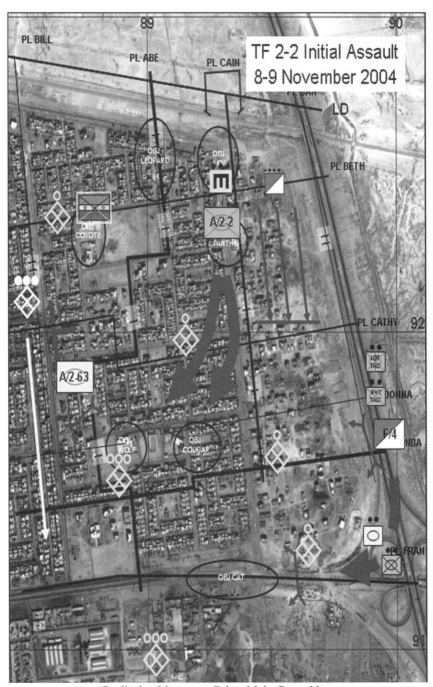

Credited to Lieutenant Colonel John Reynolds

43

lane into the city, only to be thwarted by the insurgents' defensive positions and the railroad track.[9]

A reporter for *The Christian Science Monitor* quoted a Marine officer as saying, "No plan survives the line of departure." The reporter agreed, stating:

> . . . indeed the breach plan did not. The 1-3 Marines were supposed to blow a path across train tracks, but they are well built and didn't break the first time. Then an armored bulldozer got stuck in the breach . . . With no radio and poor night-vision goggles, the backup bulldozer couldn't find the breach . . . The delay meant that several vehicles came together near the breach point. Insurgents took advantage, launching three mortars, wounding four as they struck two tanks and an armored troop carrier . . .[10]

With its breaching operation in shambles, 1/3 requested permission to use TF 2-2's breach to get its tank platoon into the city. The request was quickly granted and at 2351, the Marine tanks entered the city. While its tanks were heading into Fallujah, 1/3's medical evacuation (MEDEVACs) were using TF 2-2's breach site to evacuate the wounded. Eventually, TF 2-2 sent its M-88 to pull 1/3's stranded bulldozer out of the breach. "This was nothing new," the TF 2-2 operations officer recalled, "we'd done this before. This was a mechanized operation. We knew how to open breach sites and secure breach sites, and then we supported our sister battalion off to our right flank."[11]

TF 2-2 Commander LTC Pete Newell knew 1/3 had attempted a dismounted breach and concluded:

> You go forward, move dismounts across and clear the far side. Unfortunately, that means you can't use the big stuff to open things up with. Then the terrain was wet and hard to move in, and combined arms breaching is not something the average Marine battalion trains. It's just not a task they do, so when they gave this guy bulldozers and other stuff, they probably got them stuck. They ran into the railroad tracks and these were just things they had not anticipated.[12]

By early morning, 9 November, A/2-2 and A/2-63 began clearing to PL FRAN. Mayfield's BRT was already striking targets south of PL FRAN and the 2BN/IIF had established a strong point on OBJ TIGER. The TF 2-2 attack to PL FRAN had been expeditious and violent, killing scores of insurgents. The vicious combat also claimed the lives of the TF 2-2 command sergeant major and an American advisor to the 2BN/IIF.

At 1410 on 9 November, TF 2-2 was ordered to halt at PL FRAN and conduct search-and-attack missions north toward the LD. "The Marines were far behind schedule," Fowler explained, "and we had to cease forward momentum to allow them to catch up. This allowed the enemy to displace and reposition to the Marines' sector where they were able to move back behind our lines. We ended up forcing them out again, but we don't like to pay for ground more than once."[13]

A TF 2-2 memorandum for record (MFR) produced after the battle tried to shine the best light on the situation. "The Marine battalion, stymied due to the inherent tactical patience required by a dismounted infantry attack, caused TF 2-2 to maintain positions north of PL FRAN."[14] Newell recalled, "When we got down to Fran, and got Fran secure, we were so far ahead of the regimental combat team that, had I gone further south, it would have created a gap between us and them, and anybody who was still fighting the Marines would have just flooded the gap to get out of the way . . . I was stuck on Fran because we couldn't go until they caught up a little bit." Reynolds stated that the Marines "had a tough fight at the strongpoint . . . just across the LD."

Pointing to a map of Fallujah, Reynolds remarked, "In fact, on D+2, on the 9th, while we were on the objective (PL FRAN) early in the morning between 0700 and 0900, they were still up here. They were still fighting up here by the LD. We were already down here."[15] CNN War Correspondent Jane Arraf almost certainly captured the true mindset of TF 2-2 at the time. "I think there was a certain frustration on the part of the Army when they had to delay operations at a couple points, when the Marines were moving more slowly than they thought they'd be able to move."[16]

While the slow pace of the Marine advance may have caused some consternation within the ranks of TF 2-2, Marine indirect fire coordination received enthusiastic praise from the commander of the BRT. "The Marines actually had a good plan for indirect fires," Mayfield remembered. On 9 November, for example, one of Mayfield's BRT sections, using LRAS, observed a large group of enemy fighters running into a mosque in the 1/8 Marines' sector. The BRT executive officer began the call-for-fire procedure, asking permission to drop artillery on the mosque and shoot into the 1/8 sector. Although the request took one hour, permission was finally granted. In no time, two, 20-round missions were fired, killing more than 50 insurgents. In another similar mission, conducted by the BRT, their LRAS located enemy forces removing weapons and ammo from a building. Mayfield requested a CAS mission from the Marines. The

Marines were initially hesitant to comply as the position was in close proximity to a mosque. Not wanting to let the insurgents escape, Mayfield's men called for indirect fire onto the structure. Moments later, Marine CAS demolished the building, killing over 40 insurgents and destroying a large quantity of weapons.[17]

While this particular CAS mission was successful, TF 2-2 did experience problems coordinating CAS during the first days of battle. From his vantage point, in the TF 2-2 TOC, the assistant fire support officer, 1LT Christopher Lacour believed, "the biggest downside . . . was the [lack of] availability of Marine air for [TF] 2-2 Infantry . . ." Lacour had requested a Marine air liaison officer (ALO) for the TF 2-2 TOC prior to the fight, but did not believe the Marines could support his request. "We had maybe five air missions, with the exception of the two gun ships that were floating around at night who our Air Force guys could actually communicate with if we had priority. Not having somebody who was actually tapped into the system, who knows people in the system and how it functions, that made air not an option for us unless it was something big." Lacour explained that the Marine air "was never responsive. It took us a minimum of 30 to 40 minutes to get air assets, and we had to come into the system from the fringes . . ."[18]

The TF 2-2 commander had a firm grasp of his supporting role and saw the CAS issue in a completely different light. "Yes, it was difficult the first few days," Newell remembered. "However we were the supporting effort to the supporting effort of the division." In the end, Newell recalled, he and Tucker solved the problem with a two-minute meeting on a Fallujah rooftop.[19] Newell was quick to point out that CAS was really a nonissue with TF 2-2. "I didn't have to worry about clearing airspace because I wasn't getting any. Nor did I need it because I was moving too quick. It actually worked out very well for us."[20]

On 10 November, A/2-2 continued its search-and-attack missions north, while A/2-63 secured PL FRAN. On 11 November, TF 2-2 turned over its battle space from the LD to PL FRAN to 1/3 Marines and prepared to resume its attack south. Reynolds recalled "The [1] MAR DIV commander linked up with us at our attack position vic PL FRAN, and he was a bit surprised about our movement south (our tempo); the attack was postponed to about 1600 to facilitate 1 MAR DIV to make appropriate adjustments with other maneuver units that would potentially be in our line of fire if we moved south."[21]

At 1600, TF 2-2 once again began its assault south. As Newell's task force started its attack, 1 MAR DIV, adhering strictly to its SOP, ordered a communications security (COMSEC) change. Reynolds was adamant that, "both [he] and my staff (TOC battle crew-CPT Tom Mitchel and CPT Erik Krivda) attempted to work through RCT-7 to get the COMSEC change postponed until after the battle. A key lesson that I learned while being an OC (observer controller) at Fort Polk," Reynolds stated, "was that one should never change COMSEC hours prior to or during an attack, unfortunately I learned it again, but this time in combat."[22] In the end, Newell and Reynolds made the decision to keep their task force on their old COMSEC until the current attack ended. The TF 2-2 TOC would relay messages to RCT-7.

In the TF 2-2 TOC, however, CPT Erik Krivda, the acting executive officer for the battle, had been experiencing continual COMSEC problems with the Marines. "Yes we did have fill [load set] problems," he pointed out:

> The first fill we got from the USMC was a bad fill and caused some serious heartburn. The signal guys at 1 MAR DIV were very [resolute] on not adjusting their pattern of COMSEC changes during the battle. This meant we did a COMSEC change on the night of the 8th of November. Luckily, LTC Newell got permission not to switch our BN internal net to this fill. At the TOC, we changed fills on the regimental net and then went with the new fill, I think mid-day on the 9th. This fill on the 8th had problems and caused a lot of problems USMC wide (if I remember correctly) by the 9th there was a correction of the fill that we sent out. I know we switched about 3 or 4 days later and again there were problems with the fill that went out USMC wide.[23]

Rectifying the problems proved time consuming and difficult, albeit it did not significantly impede mission progression.

By 2000, TF 2-2 was ordered by RCT-7 to halt at PL HEATHER and wait until 1/8 Marines could catch up and pull alongside TF 2-2's western flank. At 2300, Newell's task force received permission from RCT-7 to continue its attack south. At 0600, 12 November, TF 2-2 reached its limit of advance (LOA) on PL JENNA. Upon learning from RCT-7 that any new attack south would be postponed until 1100 hours, Reynolds concluded he had time to take care of the COMSEC situation. "It was then . . . I decided to head back to Camp Fallujah with the light TAC to get the COMSEC."[24] According to Newell, "the COMSEC device with the [light] TAC was loaded with the improper COMSEC which forced them to go back to Camp Fallujah to get the right one."[25]

However, as the sun came up, major elements of Newell's command were caught in a deadly complex ambush, during which the A/2-2 executive officer was mortally wounded. According to Newell, just as the light TAC drove away:

> The insurgents came to life and started shooting. When several minutes later no one from TF 2-2 answered an RCT net call, they started checking the nets looking for us. Within minutes of that, LTC Brandl [LTC Gary Brandl] from 8th Marines dropped a radio back to the old 7th RCT fill and contacted me to remind me they were changing fills. At that moment I had literally just watched one of my tanks hit by an RPG and another skip across the ground in front of me and hit one of A/2-2's HMMWV's (the RPG did not detonate and ended up lodged in the HMMWV's back tire). Once I explained that I was in the midst of an ambush and could not change fills right away, LTC Brandl contacted 7th RCT who then dropped a radio back to the old fill to allow them to monitor our fight until we were done.[26]

With the enemy to his front and rear, and his light TAC out of the fight, Newell wisely decided to move TF 2-2 north, back to PL ISABELLA. Reynolds recalled that the first thing in Newell's mind "was the fact that we were fighting to our front and rear and he was hugely concerned with the potential for a meeting engagement between us and the 2BN/IIF and the BRT who were north of us. Had it not been for the presence of insurgents between those forces, we would have stayed where we were and fought it out."[27] The 1 MAR DIV's decision to change COMSEC in the midst of battle undoubtedly added to TF 2-2's tribulations. The FSO for TF 2-2, CPT James Cobb, recalled the situation "was the craziest and most idiotic thing I had ever heard of."[28] Newell concurred, saying that "even though we all use the same systems, changing fills is still not an easy task and with an entire task force takes time to do. Changing in the middle of a fight (which the Marines did once) is just a bad idea."[29]

From 0900, 12 November to 1100, 13 November, TF 2-2 conducted deliberate clearing operations between PL ISABELLA and PL KAREN. During this sweep, insurgents killed the A/2-2 commander, CPT Sean Sims.[30] By 1300, 13 November, TF 2-2 was ready to continue its attack south from PL JENNA. At 1330, RCT-7 delayed the LD time for TF 2-2 by two hours in order to let 1/8 Marines reach PL ISABELLA. It was not until 1500 that TF 2-2 crossed the LD to destroy remaining pockets of resistance in its zone, south of PL JENNA.

LTC Pete Newell (left) Major John Reynolds (center) and CPT James Cobb in Fallujah 13 November 2004.

By 1615, TF 2-2 had accomplished the mission and moved north to its logistics release point (LRP) to conduct a hot rearm and refuel. Newell, however, was determined to keep the enemy off balance. "What we did not want to do was stop. We just did not want to turn this into a deliberate fight, where I take a turn and then the other guy takes a turn, then I take a turn."[31] From the Army's standpoint, it appeared that the Marines would not be able to continue this tempo. "We got a call from higher on our last clearance mission that the Marines to our flank were having a lot of trouble getting in and moving south," CPT Fowler recalled.[32] During this time, Newell met with Tucker and the 1/8 Marine commanders on PL ISA-BELLA. "I went up on the roof of a building," Newell remembered, "with the commander of the [1/8] Marines and the regimental commander and did some quick coordination about where we were, where they had problems, where we were going, and then essentially attacked south again."[33]

RCT-7/TF 2-2
Passage through 1/8 Marines FLOT
13 November 2004

PL ISABELLA

PL JENNA

LRP

HOT RE-ARM/RE-FUEL – 131625

TF ASSUMES 1/8 MAR SECTOR – 131725

DEPART LOA FOR LRP – 131615

A/2-2

A/2-63

A/2-63

A/2-2

1/8

TF ATTACKS – 131745

Credited to Lieutenant Colonel John Reynolds

The plan that was constructed here called for TF 2-2 to pass through 1/8 Marines and attack south through their sector. Remarkably, Tucker and the 1/8 Marine commander did not think it would be possible. Reynolds recalled that COL Tucker and the 1/8 commander said, "No way. We can't put tanks and Bradleys down here. It's impossible." Reynolds insisted that it could, in fact, be done and remembered Newell telling the Marines, "I got it. I've been doing this all day."[34]

At 1710, TF 2-2 conducted a passage of lines through the 1/8 Marines' forward line of own troops (FLOT). With A/2-63 in the east, A/2-2 in the west, and the BRT in an ABF strong point in the southeast, TF 2-2 crossed the LD at 1720. CPT Fowler recalled the movement:

> So we all moved back north to PL ISABELLA, but shifted to our right into the 1st Battalion, 8th Marine sector: They had only cleared the first row of houses; everything south of that point was enemy-occupied territory. As we started to move into position, some marine yelled at one of my tank commanders and said 'that area's not clear, you guys can't go down there.' My TC replied with a grin, 'that's what we're here for!' We were then given the order to LD. We began moving slowly and methodically through the narrow streets that were heavily blockaded with HESCO's and T-barriers. We began to deliberately open avenues of approach with well-placed main gun rounds, using our M88 recovery vehicle to assist in the reduction of the obstacles . . . We identified strong points, PRG teams, mortar positions, and ambush sites. We walked artillery in front of us, very close, targeting areas where we received the heaviest contact. We moved quickly through the area, forcing the insurgents to flee ahead of us, and forcing them into the artillery that was falling to our south . . . They were not expecting us to break through so quickly, and it caught them off guard, once again achieving what we wanted, a breakdown or destruction of their command and control, they were in chaos . . . As we reached our southern limit of advance, we turned east, back into our own sector, planning to go through the Marines' sector again, but we had accomplished what they needed with our initial drive. We had created that hole that the Marines needed to continue their push south. So we were instructed to provide blocking positions along our boundary to prevent any insurgents from coming back into our sector.[35]

As the battle progressed, however, Fowler became more disgruntled with the Marines. "The Marines used a completely different communication system," he recalled. "It was extremely difficult to conduct adjacent unit and cross-boundary coordination because we couldn't get them on the radio because they didn't use the radio as their primary communication platform. Most coordination was done on the ground, which proved to be difficult."[36] Newell later provided a keen assessment of the difficulties associated with tank and light infantry communications:

> I have a picture in mind of a tank parked next to a building; the tank commander is unwilling to get off his vehicle to go inside because it's a pain in the butt and disconnects him from his crew. The infantryman inside the building is unwilling to go outside and stand on the tank to talk to the TC (mainly because he has never seen a tank this close and is scared to death he will shoot the cannon while he is standing there, but also because he would have to expose himself to small arms fire while he was out there). The end result is they stand 10 yards apart and yell at each other over the sounds of the fight and the whine of the tank engine.[37]

Fowler also thought RCT-7 used dated tactics and many times did not want his help. "As I was attempting to adapt our tactics to the situation, they were using the same tactics that I have studied them using in the 1960s," Fowler explained. "I offered to assist, but I guess that was insulting to them. Of course when they got in over their heads and were losing guys left and right, as well as losing ground, who did they call to pull them out? Us! On multiple occasions, our TF and in one case, just my company, had to assume the Marines sector to clear out what they could not handle."[38]

Newell offered a caveat to Fowler's assessment asserting that, "Trying to do mounted/dismounted operations on the fly, at night, and in contact just isn't easy, no matter who you are. It's even harder if you are a Marine unit that does not habitually do heavy/light operations"[39] While Newell's evaluation is unquestionably correct, Fowler's observations would prove quite similar to those of the TF 2-7 company commanders'.

As TF 2-2 fought across the chaotic urban landscape, the staff struggled to monitor the battlefield. In the TF 2-2 TOC east of the city, CPT Natalie Friel, the assistant S2 tried desperately to acquire UAV coverage from the Marines. "The Marines," she observed, "covered their own forces with their Pioneer and Shadow UAVs approximately 80-90% of the time. Our battalion had a Raven UAV, but it was virtually ineffective in the city because it could not provide an accurate 10-digit grid for targeting and it could not hover over a location. I constantly had to beg and plead with the Marines via e-mail, phone and Microsoft chat to get their UAV over [to] our sector." In the end, Friel reported, "Our UAV coverage became so minimal that I actually requested the 3BCT/1ID from Baqubah send me one of their Shadow UAVs."[40] Since TF 2-2 was the supporting effort in the operation, they were clearly not the Marines' top priority for UAV coverage. It would appear however, that the intensity of the fighting in the Marine sectors forced them to severely limit UAV coverage for TF 2-2.

Another problem in the TOC was communications. CPT Krivda was concerned that he could not reposition his TOC for fear of losing connectivity with the Marines:

> We would have liked to move the TOC . . . the problem was just connection with the Marine Corps. That was our big fear, that we would lose connectivity . . . We had a landline phone, not a TA-312, but we normally used it just as regular DSN (defense switched network) line. But the problem was that our version of that phone was a newer version and was not compatible with the Marine Corps' version of the DSN phone. So, if we picked up the phone to talk to the G4 or the regimental 4, we couldn't talk. So, we had to get a Marine Corps version of it and be tied in [to a] landline to the other Marine battalions and tied into the Marine regimental headquarters that way. So, therefore, we were limited in how we could move.

One other major difficulty identified in the TF 2-2 TOC was the Marines use of Microsoft Chat. Krivda reported:

> The other major factor was that they [RCT-7] used a Microsoft Chat to do a lot of their instant messaging, even between battalions, the regiment and division. In some aspects, it was really great, particularly for intel. We could get a lot of information fast; disseminate it, print and save it and a lot of spot reports, we could keep from different sectors, whether it was 1/3 or 1/8 Marines. So, we could inform our guys of what was going on. The problem was that the Marines have some kind of wireless capability that they could put [in] their TAC out north of Fallujah and still talk off the Internet laptop. We just didn't have that capability. We had set up a satellite system that would tie in that way. It was mounted out of two Humvees, basically. We could mount it on a roof if we were in an abandoned building, and that's where we basically stayed the whole time. The TAC could move back and forth but, again, with the majority of regimental communications not on FM traffic, it was on this instant messenger stuff; the regimental traffic was very quiet. So that was something that was difficult to keep up with. We did update a lot on FM, but a lot different than the Marines did. So we would take it off Blue Force Tracker and we would update it at the TOC and send it forward to the regiment. Or, every now and then, they would call or the regimental com-

mander would come into sector and talk face to face with Lieutenant Colonel Newell.[41]

Jeff Jager, the former LNO and Assistant S3, knew about the Marine chat capability, but did not realize until well into the fight that the Marines were using it in their TAC:

> I didn't understand that they had the ability to position that asset forward in a tactical command post or a forward command and control element, but that's what they had. I'm not sure what system it was or how they did it, but the RCT-7 FM command net was a pretty quiet net. We were pretty much the only people that talked on it, because the RCT conducted command and control over chat . . . But we didn't have that ability forward with us. I think that's one of the things that, had I recognized that fact earlier, it would have paid huge dividends for us in the fight . . . We couldn't monitor what the other battalions were telling the RCT because they didn't call them on the FM net; they told them on SIPR chat. We had the ability to monitor that SIPR chat back at our TOC in Fallujah, but the only effective system we had to transmit messages from the TOC at Camp Fallujah to the TAC-which is where the colonel and S3 were forward was the Blue Force Tracker. This is a good system but slow . . . Even though our TOC and TAC were only separated by less than 10 kilometers, we had almost no FM communications between them. There was something that caused the radios not to work very well. The TOC had situational awareness at the RCT level but I would say the TAC didn't have it as good as it should have, had I figured out that we needed that SIPR chat system forward.[42]

While there were communication problems between RCT-7 and TF 2-2, the communications between Tucker and Newell were exceptionally good. Almost every day, in the late afternoon, Tucker appeared at Newell's heavy TAC:

> He would show up and we'd pull out the plexi-glassed-over imagery with the block map on it . . . That's how we kind of adjusted phase lines and CFLs [coordinated fire lines], was by saying, "Hey I'm going to push into this block and this block and this block. I need to move the division CFL a little further over here . . ." We did this from my TAC, from the front of a Humvee. That really became the TTP [tactics, techniques, and procedures] for every plan we put together. We'd essentially, with him standing there, sketch out a course of action of what we intended on doing. Then he and his S-3 would go back to the regimental TOC and then sketch out the regimental plan

that supported that. The regiment essentially wrote the orders to support us, but where we went, they followed.[43]

From 14 to 16 November, TF 2-2 conducted clearing and quick reaction missions in the RCT-7 sector. On 17 and 18 November, Newell's men cleared the industrial sector of caches and IEDs. The task force conducted an attack-to-clear mission south of Fallujah on 19 November and on 20 November, performed a battle hand off with 1/8 Marines and pulled out of Fallujah.

In nearly two weeks of fighting, TF 2-2 killed more than 304 insurgents and went from the supporting effort to the main effort in RCT-7's sector. According to Reynolds, "the RCT [7] commander didn't know how 2-2 came from being the supporting effort to being the main effort. It happened so quickly."[44] Although minor problems did occur during the course of the battle, Tucker and Newell overcame the challenges by meeting daily on the battleground, effectively circumventing any command and control problems.

Although victorious on the battlefield, TF 2-2 did pay a price. In the end, Newell's command suffered seven killed in action (KIA) and 72 wounded in action (WIA).[45] Due in great measure to the Marines precise

COL Craig Tucker (right) and MAJ John Reynolds (center) during Operation AL FAJR.

control features and coordination, no one in TF 2-2 or RCT-7 was killed or wounded by friendly fire.

RCT-1/TF 2-7 Joint Assault into Fallujah

At 1400, 8 November, Marine air attempted to establish a viable breach into the city by blasting the railroad berm to the west of the Fallujah train station, using eight, 2,000-pound bombs. Soon thereafter, Marine D9 bull-dozers began cutting two holes through the berm. At approximately 1900, 3/1 Marines captured the train station, which enabled them to provide cover fire for Marine engineers moving toward the breach site with their MCLICs. Once at the breach site, the engineers fired their MCLICs into a field to the south in order to cut two lanes through the enemy minefield. Unfortunately, these efforts provided little help. RCT-1 was still having difficulty. Shupp recalled, "the tracks have to be cut because the vehi-cles were getting stuck in the railroad tracks. So, the engineers take eight charges (one pound sticks of TNT) and blow up the railroad tracks: four across the top, four across the bottom, and then push that aside. Now we have two lanes."[46]

In its attack positions north of Fallujah, LTC James Rainey's TF 2-7 waited in the dark for the breach to be completed. "We were staged, wait-ing for the breach to get put in," Rainey remembered, "and they had some troubles with just the normal fog and friction of combat. So, we were waiting about four to six hours, trying to keep everybody alert. We were frustrated, as you can imagine, because we were burning that darkness up and we really wanted to have the entire period of darkness-limited vis-ibility to fight."[47]

"It was raining," the TF 2-7 S3, MAJ Tim Karcher, remembered, "and it was a really miserable evening. We sat there for a good six or seven hours waiting to go, watching this rain of fire down on the city. We watched this death and destruction rain down on the city, from AC-130s to any kind of fast-moving aircraft, 155 [millimeter] howitzers. You name it, everybody was getting in the mix."[48]

C/3-8 Commander CPT Peter Glass, whose company would lead the way in to Fallujah, grew concerned. "Those train tracks presented a seri-ous obstacle for vehicles that have suspension, mainly my tanks. If we had gone up against those, we would have broken several road wheels making the mission inoperable."[49]

CPT Edward Twaddell III, whose A/2-7 was assigned the mission of capturing the Jolan Park, recounted, "We were pretty close and, as you're well aware, MCLCs will make a big boom. I don't recall hearing it detonate. I'm not saying they didn't use it. I did not hear a MCLC go off, but then again, maybe it went off and I wasn't paying attention or maybe I confused it with an aircraft strike or something like that."[50]

Finally, at 0130, 9 November, almost six and a half hours after TF 2-2 attacked in the east, TF 2-7 crossed the LD. Unfortunately, there was still no lane for Rainey's men and machines. "We actually didn't get through the breach until 0130 and there wasn't a lane, so [C/3-8's] lead tank . . . led with a roller," Rainey remembered. Not only did the roller open the lane; it also proved an effective marker. According to Rainey:

> I remember doing breaches at the National Training Center (NTC) as a younger officer thinking, 'When the hell are we ever going to do this shit?' So we rolled the lane, [and] marked it. The rollers went through the open area and hit the main road, and the breach was easy to find because the kid who was doing it just jammed the rollers right into the wall on the other side of the road. To get a roller off the tank, you have to dismount the tank in contact to get the roller off, because you can't turn with it. He gets out and drops the roller. Now we've got a lane marked and we've got a good point to orient on because the roller's stuck in the wall on the other side of the road.[51]

Apparently, a disconnect occurred between Shupp and Rainey regarding the existence of the lane. While Shupp was convinced his Marines had created a lane, Rainey was equally sure they had not. It may be that the confusion arose from a disparity in what constituted a lane. It was CPT Fowler from TF 2-2, who noted during the planning phase of the operation that the Army and Marines used some of the same terminology, but that "it meant different things to them than to us."[52]

Surprised they had not received any enemy fire as they pushed through the breach, Glass' C/3-8 roared east on the northern-most road, and then turned south on PL HENRY.[53] Following behind C/3-8, Twaddell's A/2-7 was the next company through the breach. Once on the northern road, Twaddell lined his company up on the three avenues of advance and began the attack in zone toward the Jolan Park.[54]

Slowly bringing up the rear of TF 2-7 was CPT Chris Brooke's C/2-7. "We'd move a couple hundred yards and then stop and then move again," Brooke related:

Once we got to the breach, it became very clear as to what happened. It was absolute chaos. There was a sea of Humvees from the Marines in position to go through the breach, and every one of them had a chem light on their antenna! I don't know why they did it, because we were looking for chem lights that were marking the breach sites, so it was just chaos. My first platoon leader, who was ahead of us, was at one point dismounted and going up to people and asking them which way the breach was. We finally negotiated our way through there without event, and once we did get up there it was clearly marked and it was fine.[55]

Like 1/3 Marines in the RCT-7 sector, RCT-1's breaching operation was, at best, confused.

As Glass' C/3-8 turned south down PL HENRY, they came under sporadic RPG and small-arms fire. The company used their .50 caliber and coax machine guns to destroy IEDs and decimate the enemy encountered along the way.

Meanwhile, A/2-7 pushed rapidly south toward Jolan Park. During the advance, they met with "very light resistance throughout the evening," according to Twaddell. "Although there were several folks that tried to go stand out in the middle of the street with an AK-47 and face down a Bradley, it ended badly for them," he recollected.[56]

Shupp believed the delay at the breach actually worked out well for RCT-1. With the enemy focused on RCT-7's attack in the northeast and on the bridge sites to the west, Shupp was convinced, "This is an area the enemy never expects anyone to attack in, and [we] are having tremendous success."[57]

As Twaddell's A/2-7 closed in on Jolan Park and began taking fire, TF 2-7 and RCT-1 pounded enemy locations with CAS and 120-millimeter mortars. "We were able to really leverage the fires," Twaddell recalled.[58] Shupp would later point out that at about this time he met with Rainey and both men "were just shocked at the success we're having."[59]

With the sun coming up, Twaddell's company blasted its way into Jolan Park. Attacking through the objective, Twaddell dismounted his infantry and began to clear back north. The action "totally devastated the enemy," Rainey remembered. "They were still trying to get out of the way of the tanks and Bradleys and our infantry squads were on top of them."[60]

Sergeant First Class (SFC) John Urrutia, 2d platoon sergeant for A/2-7, stated that the infantry did not dismount until they reached Jolan Park:

> . . . that was the first time we actually dismounted, and that was to clear the market area. Now, attached to our platoon were two Marine engineers, a lance corporal and a PFC. They had about 20 pounds of C4, which really came in handy as we got into the market . . . Once we got into this market, we started to blow holes through these concrete walls to work our way in there, and that's where our engineers played a vital role in helping us.[61]

Urrutia pointed out that the Marine engineers were a great asset to his company. "The lance corporal was like, 'Hey, wherever you need me.'" he recalled.[62] Reaffirming their commitment to the joint fight, the Marines task organized their engineer assets down to TF 2-7's platoons.

Alpha 2-7 continued to take rocket, mortar, RPG, and small-arms fire in Jolan Park as they waited for 3/1 Marines to arrive and conduct a passage of lines. At one point, a 127-millimeter rocket landed on a building, resulting in six American casualties. Rainey thought that the 3/1 Marines were not moving as quickly as planned, but was quick to point out that "3/1 still had a tough fight behind us rooting those guys out."[63]

By most accounts, 3/1's passage of lines through TF 2-7 was something to behold. According to Rainey:

> . . . the only good thing that came out of the delay with the breach taking an extra four hours was that now it was daylight and that was better than doing the passage in darkness. It's hard enough doing a forward passage of lines in contact . . . But now, you've got a U.S. Army unit doing a passage of lines with a Marine unit in contact, so this is about as complex an operation as you can get going here . . . Captain Twaddell had guys in contact so Major Karcher and I decided that that was the decisive point in the battle. We bounded up to Phase Line Henry three or four blocks over to Jolan Park and linked up with Captain Twaddell, who was doing a great job with the passage of lines. I told him to get back in the fight and concentrate on the enemy. Major Karcher, our S3, and the 3/1 S3 dismounted and the two of them stood on the corner talking on the radios. After a little bit of friction, they managed to complete the passage of lines and we got contact points set up. The challenge of doing a passage of lines is always finding the lanes. You've got to use what works for you, but in an urban environment, the lanes are the roads . . . So we got them on about four lanes and turned to the west. 3/1, over the course of about four hours, passes about two of their companies through us and

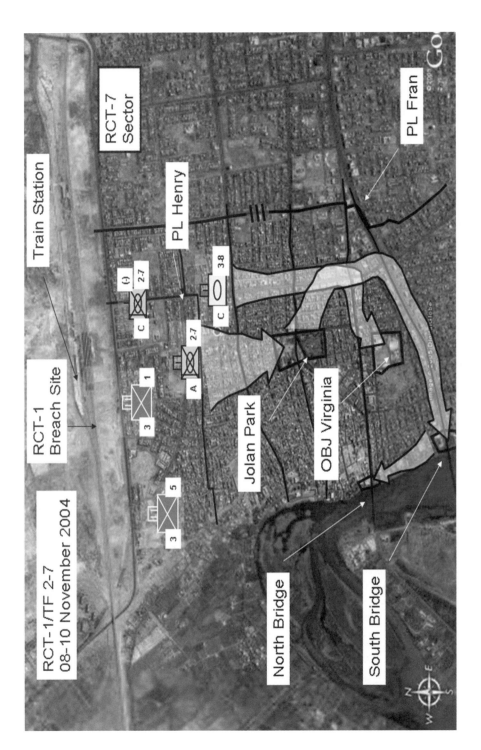

RCT-1/TF 2-7
08–10 November 2004

RCT-1
Breach Site

Train Station

RCT-7
Sector

PL Henry

PL Fran

3 5
3

3 1

A 2-7

C (-) 2-7

C 3-8

Jolan Park

OBJ Virginia

North Bridge

South Bridge

N
W E
S

From the collection of Sergeant First Class John Urrutia

COL Michael Shupp Commander RCT-1 (left) and LTC James Rainey Commander TF 2-7.

got turned down to the west, which then freed up Apache [A/2-7] to consolidate and complete actions on the objective and secure Jolan Park.[64]

Karcher was convinced that "[TF] 2-7 wasn't much in the way of clearing; we were in the mode of destroying. So, the Marines actually went in and did the dirty work of clearing, and I've got to give them credit for that. They were awesome, but they took a lot of casualties in the process."[65]

By 1230, 9 November, A/2-7 had completed the passage of lines with 3/1 Marines. While RCT-1 planners thought it would take 24 hours for TF 2-7 to secure the Jolan Park, Rainey's men managed to secure the objective in a mere 12 hours.[66]

On the night of 9 November, Rainey pushed C/3-8 down PL HENRY and then rolled the company west, down PL FRAN, (also known as Highway 10), headed for OBJ VIRGINIA. Rainey described OBJ VIRGINIA as an "open schoolyard-looking piece of terrain." In the interim, Chris Brooke's C/2-7 moved down PL HENRY, securing the lines of communications.[67]

Once on OBJ VIRGNIA, Glass' company spotted 10 to 20 insurgents in a building near a mosque to the west. Fearful indirect fire or CAS would damage the mosque, Rainey, Karcher, and Glass were conflicted as to

61

how to proceed. Suddenly, LTC Ron Lewis, the Commander of the 1st Battalion, 227th Aviation Regiment (1-227) came up on the net. As the organic attack battalion for the 4th Aviation Brigade, 1st Cavalry Division (4BCT/1CD), 1-227 had been tasked to support RCT-1's main effort. Lewis recommended firing two laser-guided Hellfire missiles into the building. Rainey concurred and set about clearing the area, whereupon the AH-64D blew the building to bits, killing everyone inside.[68]

Looking back on his unit's actions in Fallujah, COL James C. Mc-Conville, Commander of 4BCT/1CD said he felt there were no problems integrating with the Marines. "It was important, though," he remembered, "for us to understand their procedures even though they were a little different, because it was their airspace. Our philosophy was: when they were in Army airspace over 1st CAV, they followed our procedures; so now that we're in their airspace, we'll follow their procedures. We really didn't have a lot of problems."[69]

With 3/1 Marines still slugging it out with the insurgents in the Jolan District and 3/5 Marines fighting in the northwest corner of the city, Rainey called Shupp and told him he could either continue his attack or consolidate his position. Shupp immediately ordered Rainey to continue the attack.[70]

Rainey promptly ordered his men forward. At 0900, 10 November, Twaddell's A/2-7 began its push to the key bridge sites on the Euphrates River. At the northern-most bridge, Twaddell ran into Marines moving toward his company from the east. "We came nose to nose with a Marine company," Twaddell recalled. "They were fighting from east to west and we were coming right up into their area from the south. So we did our recon as quickly as we could and got out of their hair . . ."[71] By the morning of 11 November, A/2-7 moved back to the task force support area and prepared for a new mission.

By that same morning, the Marines reached PL FRAN. According to Rainey, "The Marines [were] having a good, but tough fight. They had some casualties, but they're rooting out the last pockets of the enemy in the 1st RCT sector . . . So it took them about 48 hours."[72] The ferocity of the battle proved costly for the Marines. Shupp remembered 3/1 Marines taking 20 to 30 KIA in the first 48 hours.[73]

The 3/1 Marines also took a substantial number of WIA. Fortunately for the Marines, TF 2-7 was prepared to assist. "His [Rainey's] battalion

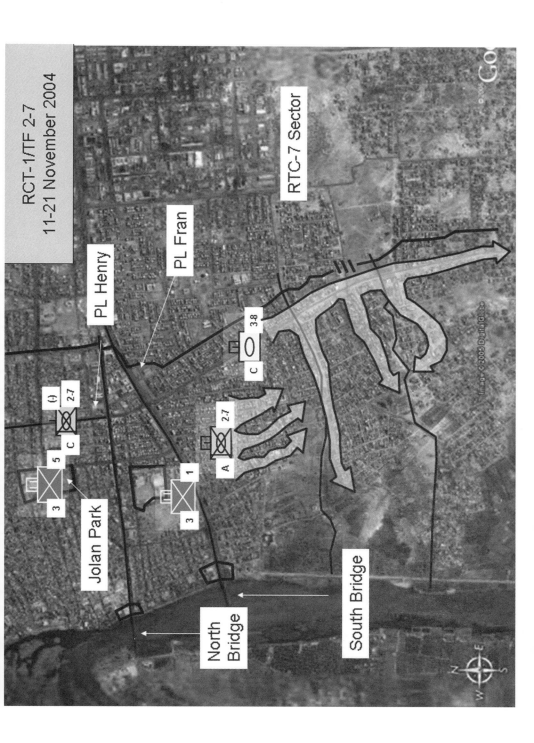

RCT-1/TF 2-7
11-21 November 2004

PL Henry

PL Fran

RTC-7 Sector

3-8

C

(-) 2-7

C

5

3

2-7

A

1

3

Jolan Park

North Bridge

South Bridge

63

aid station [was] co-located with 3/1's battalion aid station," Shupp explained, "and the Army armored MEDEVACs are a godsend on the battlefield because, in the Marine Corps, we don't have any armored evacuation.[74] The Marines did in fact possess the AAVP7A1 (assault amphibian vehicle personnel), but they were hesitant to bring the troop carrier into the city. "It's got the armor plating of most good desks," Karcher explained. "It's a very lightly armored vehicle; having said that, they were reluctant to bring those into the city, and rightfully so."[75]

As the battle progressed, Shupp grew increasingly impressed with TF 2-7's 120-millimeter mortars. "Our 60- and [81] millimeter mortars are great to go ahead and attack the enemy out in the open and hit him on the rooftops, but our Marines found out that when you take an Army 120-millimeter mortar and drop it on the top of a building, it's dropping the floor."[76] At times during the battle in the RCT-1 sector, TF 2-7 allowed Marine FSOs to use its 120-millimeter mortars. Task Force 2-7 FSO, CPT Coley D. Tyler, remembered, "We used our mortars and also the Marines used our mortars quite a bit. Of course, the Marines only had 60-millimeter mortars and 81s. So anytime 2-7 wasn't using our 120s, we just passed them over to the Marines and let them shoot. We ended up, through the course of two weeks, firing almost 1,000 rounds."[77] With its tanks, Bradleys, armored ambulances, and heavy mortars, TF 2-7 was quickly proving its worth to the Marines.

In the early morning hours of 11 November, MG Richard F. Natonski, the 1 MAR DIV commander, met with Shupp and Rainey on PL HENRY. The topic of the meeting or "quick huddle" as Rainey called it, was to discuss the possibility of sending TF 2-7 into RCT-7's sector. Rainey told Natonski "it was not easy to break contact, disengage get back and go get integrated in a new regimental combat team, so I offered the suggestion of just continuing the attack south along Phase Line Henry."[78] Natonski and Shupp spoke briefly and made the decision to continue the attack south with TF 2-7.

From 11 to 13 November, TF 2-7 continued its attack south, with C/3-8 moving down PL HENRY, A/2-7 attacking south from PL FRAN and C/2-7 guarding the LOC. Rainey pointed out that "this was not a clearance mission, but we did pick some zones where we thought the enemy was concentrated based on the terrain and intelligence."[79]

On 12 November, an antitank round penetrated the ramp of CPT Twaddell's Bradley. The round sheared off the arm of one soldier on the track

Major General Natonski (center) and members of TF 2-2 staff during Operation AL FAJR.

and passed through an Iraqi interpreter, killing him instantly. Several other individuals inside the Bradley also sustained injuries. The following day, nearly an entire squad in A/2-7 was wounded in a deadly firefight which claimed the life of Specialist (SPC) Jose Velez.[80] In C/3-8, SGT Jonathan Shields was killed when his tank flipped over in a large crater. The company suffered WIAs from RPGs which shattered the tank's vision blocks and nearly killed a tank commander. In another case, an RPG fired from a building penetrated a loader's hatch, wounding the loader.[81] Through it all, TF 2-7 continued to pummel the insurgents. "It was just unbelievable heroism and bravery," Rainey declared.[82]

Like the men and women in the TF 2-2 TOC, the staff of TF 2-7 labored to monitor the battlefield. CPT Michael Erwin recalled that their TOC used both the Raven UAV and the Marine Scan Eagle UAV. "We had a terminal for that in our TOC, we really had two different UAV platforms going at the same time . . . We were definitely not the priority for that. Once we breached the city and led the way in, we no longer became the priority for that."[83]

According to Erwin, communication with the Marines was not a serious problem:

The Marines rely heavily on TACSAT radio and mIRC Chat. We did not have the ability to establish much of a secret Internet protocol router network (SIPRNET) out there due to our location and how quickly we had to set up. So, there were definitely issues talking on the radios between the Marines and us, just due to the fact that we really, almost unfailingly, use FM, and the first time I experienced TACSAT was down in Najaf. Although it was a bit of a challenge, it was nothing we were not able to work through . . . I think we learned about teamwork working with the Marines. I think a lot of people were under the impression that it was going to be hard for an Army unit to work with the Marines, with their different radio communications, different attack aviation assets, and different sizes in companies [and] lots of little things.[84]

Task Force 2-7 also faced problems with COMSEC similar to those encountered by TF 2-2, though Shupp believed the issue was never a serious problem:

We had NIPRNET (non-secure Internet protocol router network) and SIPRNET challenges that we had to work through on the battlefield to exchange data and to exchange e-mails, but believe it or not, there were many times I could not reach Jim [Rainey] because of VHF problems, but I could e-mail with him . . . And we would be able to exchange e-mails and talk to each other. Either Karcher and myself or Jim Rainey were able to talk on the Internet without problems. There were some problems with the fills since we were working off different fill devices, but that was something that was easily overcome. We just needed to let our S6 work those problems out for us, but it was never a showstopper.[85]

From 14 November until 19 November, TF 2-7 conducted attacks in support of 3/1 Marines. During much of this time frame, however, the TF 2-7 company commanders became increasingly irritated by their role, convinced they were being held back and used primarily as route security.

"I'm not privy to what was going on at the regimental level or above that," Twaddell remarked, "but we all felt, we've got a mechanized task force that is sitting still. Meanwhile, we're listening to radio reports and hearing about great Marines getting hurt, not through any fault of their own, but they didn't have the protection afforded by armored vehicles. So we were very frustrated. It appeared that the whole force was not using the assets available to accomplish the mission."[86]

CPT Brooke was also concerned:

Once we had killed all of our targets and Henry was secure, we just wanted to get back into the fight and help these guys out. We were ei-

TF 2-7 soldiers in Fallujah.

From the collection of Sergeant First Class John Urrutia-

ther doing casualty evacuations for these guys (throwing their young Marines in the backs of our Bradleys), or we're watching their casualty evacuations going past us on the street. All we want to do is get in there and help out. 'Put me in, coach,' I remember, at one point, I was on the net and told a Marine company commander that I could give him a platoon of Bradleys and where did he want me to go. He said just hold Henry and they had the fight, which was frustrating for us. I didn't know what his tactical situation was on the ground and this is all post-game commentary now; but that was very frustrating to have so much firepower sitting there waiting and ready and capable of being used, and there was no reason why we couldn't have been used to help those guys out. In one case, some Marines were taking significant fire early in the fight and I sent down one of my platoons to suppress. We unloaded our ready boxes into a building on the south side there. They were in the process of trying to work a fire mission and we were able to assist there, which was great, but we wish we could have continued to do that.[87]

According to Twaddell, CPT Glass was also concerned. "It seemed that 3-8 was also being held back," Twaddell explained. "Pete Glass, he was an amazing commander. He was all about taking the fight to the enemy and we were all frustrated."[88]

The S3 for TF 2-7, MAJ Karcher, saw the issue somewhat differently. He remembered guarding ROUTE HENRY and isolating the enemy during the last week or so of the operation, while the Marines performed house-to-house clearing operations. "The Marines were taking far greater casualties than we thought were necessary or required," Karcher pointed out. "So, in conjunction with their commander and their S3, my commander and I talked to those folks and said, 'Hey look, we can do some stuff for you. If you'll tell us what your ops are for tomorrow, before the sun comes up we can just drive through there, attempt to draw out any fire and destroy some of those strong points before you have to send men in first.'" In Karcher's opinion, the Marines took full advantage of this process, but had to be prodded into doing so. Karcher believed the Marines needed a nudge, "Not because they were dumb, but because they were using the assets they had. We were like, 'Hey, we're not doing enough. Instead of you taking it in the face on the way in the door, we can leave nothing but a charred room.'" Karcher recalled that TF 2-7 helped 3/1 Marines with their clearing operations for three or four days, which proved highly successful. The 3/1 Marine S3 was elated with TF 2-7's contribution to the fight, stating, "We went into the buildings and there was nothing but freaking dead insurgents in there." Karcher remembered thinking, "It was a good feeling .

. . ."[89] At noon on 20 November, TF 2-7 withdrew from Fallujah. During the ferocious combat, Rainey's unit suffered two KIA and the loss of six tanks and three or four Bradleys.

Shupp was convinced that TF 2-7 had performed magnificently in Fallujah, and was shocked that a popular book about the battle failed to mention their contributions and achievements. "It's terrible," Shupp stated, "because the true heroes of that fight were not mentioned. They're all my sons, and 2-7 was incredible. No one can ever take that away from them. We could not have had that success if it wasn't for that Army battalion: their mortars, their maintenance, their fighting capability inside that city."[90]

In the end, Rainey praised the Marines for their gallant efforts and maintained that in order to clear and secure a city the size of Fallujah, dismounted infantry would always be needed. He was equally certain that if the objective required destroying the enemy and capturing key terrain in a city, a heavy force could be highly successful. "I believe that not only can you do that mounted with mechanized forces, [but] you can also do it faster, with more effect on the enemy and [with] way fewer casualties by going with that mounted tank and Bradley/dismounted infantry mix, as long as you have fire support." Rainey was quick to point out that this model was Iraq, and that the lessons learned in Fallujah might not apply against a different enemy.[91] Rainey's assessment may have fallen on deaf ears. In 2005, Marine Commandant, GEN Michael W. Hagee, told an audience in Quantico, Virginia that, "In my opinion, Fallujah is an example of what we're going to fight in the future, and not a bad example of how to fight it . . . it is about individual Marines with small arms going house to house, killing. We may not want to say that, but that's what it is about."[92]

The Army's withdrawal from Fallujah did not end the fighting. The Marines continued to weed out and kill the few remaining die-hard insurgents for weeks after the Army's departure. In the end, Operation AL FAJR proved to be a tremendous joint tactical success, and although there were problems, neither service denied the bravery and commitment of the other.

Notes

1. "F/4 Operation PHANTOM FURY History of Events," copy in author's possession
2. Reynolds; "TF 2-2 Infantry, Operation PHANTOM FURY (summary)", copy in author's possession.
3. CPT Jeff Jager, telephone interview by author, 17 May 2006. "Interestingly, A/2-63 recovered the first raven (intact) somewhere in the city hours later." LTC Newell, e-mail interview by author, 7 June 2006.
4. CPT Paul A. Fowler, "Memorandum for Record, Narrative of Combat Actions in Fallujah from 4 to 23 November 2004, 25 November 2004, copy in author's posession.
5. MAJ Lisa DeWitt, telephone interview by author, 23 April 2006.
6. "Narrative: Recommendation For Award of the Silver Star to CPT Sean P. Sims," copy in author's possession.
7. CPT Paul Fowler, e-mail interview by author, 4 April 2006.
8. Ibid.
9. "Narrative: Recommendation for CPT Sean P. Sims."
10. Scott Peterson, "US Forces Pour into Iraqi City," The Christian Science Monitor, 10 November 2004.
11. Reynolds.
12. Newell, telephone interview by author, 10 March 2006.
13. Fowler, e-mail interview.
14. "Memorandum For Record, Subject: Task Force 2d Battalion 2d Infantry Regiment Operation Phantom Fury, 02 January 2005," copy in author's file.
15. Reynolds.
16. Arraf interview.
17. Mayfield, e-mail interview by author, 9 March 2006.
18. CPT Christopher Lacour, telephone interview by author, 15 May 2006.
19. Newell, e-mail interview by author, 13 February 2006.
20. Newell, telephone interview by author, 23 March 2006.
21. Reynolds.
22. Ibid.
23. CPT Erik Krivda, e-mail interview by author, 26 May 2006.
24. Reynolds, e-mail interview by author, 27 May 2006.
25. Newell, e-mail interview by author, 1 June 2006.
26. Ibid.
27. Reynolds, e-mail interview by author, 31 May 2006.
28. Captain James Cobb, telephone interview by author, 2 June 2006.
29. Newell, email interview by author, 22 March 2006.
30. Newell, telephone interview; Reynolds; TF 2-2 IN Operation Phantom Fury Summary.
31. Newell.
32. CPT Paul A. Fowler, "Memorandum For Record."
33. Newell, telephone interview

34. Reynolds, interview.
35. CPT Paul A. Fowler, "Memorandum for Record, Narrative of Combat Actions in Fallujah 4 to 23 November 2004, 25 November 2004."
36. Fowler.
37. Newell, e-mail interview by author, 6 June 2006.
38. Fowler.
39. Newell, e-mail interview by author, 12 June 2006.
40. CPT Natalie Friel, e-mail interview by author, 10 March 2006.
41. Krivda.
42. CPT Jeff Jager, telephone interview by author, 17 May 2006.
43. Newell, telephone interview.
44. Reynolds.
45. 1LT Gregory D. McCrum, "Lessons Learned: Medical Employment During the Battle for Fallujah," (No Date)
46. Ibid.
47. LTC James Rainey, telephone interview by author, 19 April 2006.
48. Karcher.
49. CPT Peter Glass, telephone interview by author, 29 March 2006.
50. CPT Edward Twaddell III, telephone interview by author, 28 February 2006.
51. Rainey.
52. CPT Paul Fowler, e-mail interview by author, 4 April 2006.
53. Glass.
54. Twaddell; Rainey.
55. CPT Chris Brooke, telephone interview with author, 1 May 2006.
56. Twaddell.
57. Shupp.
58. Rainey.
59. Shupp.
60. Rainey.
61. SFC John Urrutia, interviewed by author at Fort Leavenworth, 14 March 2006.
62. Ibid.
63. Rainey.
64. Ibid.
65. Karcher
66. Ibid.
67. Rainey.
68. Ibid.
69. COL James C. McConville, telephone interview by author, 21 April 2006.
70. Ibid.
71. Twaddell.
72. Rainey.
73. Shupp.

74. Ibid.

75. Karcher.

76. Ibid.

77. CPT Coley D. Tyler, telephone interview by author, 20 April 2006.

78. Rainey.

79. Ibid.

80. Twaddell; Rainey.

81. Glass.

82. Rainey

83. Erwin.

84. Ibid.

85. Shupp.

86. Twaddell.

87. Brooke; In some regards, Brooke's assessment contains shades of the Army and Marine action in Obong-ni Korea in August 1950. Dr. William Glenn Robertson, Counterattack on the Naktong, 1950, (Leavenworth: Combat Studies Institute, December, 1985), 83-102.

88. Twaddell.

89. Karcher.

90. Shupp.

91. Rainey.

92. Thomas E. Ricks, Fiasco, (New York: The Penguin Press, 2006), 405.

Chapter 4

Conclusions

*None of the service parochialisms existed out there. It was an unbeliev-
able mutual respect for one another on the battlefield.*

LTG General John F. Sattler, US Marines

While Operation AL FAJR stands as an indisputable joint success, it
was not without its share of difficulties, complexities, and challenges. A
list of the problems encountered, in descending order of importance, includes communications, equipment, breaching operations, intelligence,
and perception issues.

Communication problems presented perhaps the most significant of
all the difficulties between the Army and Marines in the battle of Fallujah.
Although TF 2-7 and TF 2-2 had minimal problems communicating on the
battlefield, TF 2-7 did note "the challenges of communicating with joint
services" in their AAR.[1] TF 2-7's AAR noted the Army used FM, Force
XXI Battle Command, Brigade and Below (FBCB2), and Blue Force
Tracker (BFT), whereas the Marines used tactical satellite radio (TAC-
SAT), mIRC, Internet Relay Chat (mIRC CHAT), and command and control for the PC (C2PC).[2] At the very least, these competing systems caused
friction, and were not fielded to all the units in the battle space. Simply
stated, the Army and Marines did not always rely on the same communication equipment. CPT Pete Glass, the C/3-8 Commander, recalled, "There
were a couple times when it got hairy and there were a couple close calls
with blue on blue, or fratricide, just because the common operating picture
between the Army and the Marines is not there. I think if coalition forces
are going to continue to do operations like this, we need to have a broad
spectrum where everybody shares the same stuff, has the same picture and
the same FBCB2, Blue Force Tracker, so we can continue to do operations
and functions like this."[3] Staff Sergeant (SSG) David Bellavia, a squad
leader in TF 2-2, recalled major communication problems as his unit assaulted into Fallujah. "We got right up to the edge of the city and some
idiot is bleeding over on our company net, and it's a Marine. I hear CPT
Sims lose his mind, and then I hear our own platoon lose their mind, were
on a fighter net . . . My radio guy . . . is ready to refill my radio, I said,

'What the hell is going on?' They said the Marines washed us out and told us to get off the net. We had to do a communications security (COMSEC) changeover."[4]

TF 2-7's S3, MAJ Tim Karcher, did not believe there were problems communicating with the Marines in Fallujah, because of his unit's experience in Najaf.[5] Unlike TF 2-2, which experienced difficulties with load sets and fill devices, TF 2-7 did not, in fact, experience serious problems with COMSEC. Interestingly, TF 2-2 made no comments concerning communication problems in their AAR.[6]

Apparently, the most significant problems with communications occurred at the company level where Army company commanders found it difficult, if not occasionally impossible, to communicate with adjacent Marine companies. According to LTC Newell, Marine companies adjacent to his companies "changed constantly. Had we had more time to plan and rehearse I probably would have insisted that [my company commanders] go to the 3d Marines' rehearsal and that the adjacent Marine company commanders attend ours, but I'm not sure that would have completely alleviated the problem."[7]

While obstacles arising from the most basic organizational deficiencies were rare, nonetheless, they did occur. TF 2-7's AAR concluded, "Army medical capability far exceeds Marine capability at battalion level."[8] It is a troubling reality that the Marines lacked armored ambulances, a fact that could place not only the wounded at greater risk, but those charged with transporting them as well. This incongruity was not lost on Army personnel who observed the dangerous trek as the Marines continually carried their wounded out of the city in HMMWV's. RCT-1's casualties might indeed have been greater if not for TF 2-7's offer to transport wounded Marines by way of their own armored ambulances and Bradleys. This sprit of solidarity continued at the aid station, where according to CSM Mace, "They [the Marines] were taking more casualties than we were. The commander wanted to make our guys more responsive and he said, 'Okay, let's help out the Marines.' So we pushed part of our medics forward. I don't know if they treated any Army right there at the Marine aid station, but they treated a heck of a lot of Marines . . ."[9]

1LT Chris Boggiano, an officer in TF 2-2, probably captured the true essence of the Marine Corps' equipment problems:

> My second reconnaissance was my first interaction with the Marines, when we were setting up the staging area and the Marines, by that

point, had cordoned off the city. They were all sitting up on the berm, on the highway, and they're shooting and shooting and we're not seeing any tracer rounds coming back at them so Captain Mayfield wanted me to find out what was going on. So, I drove up there with the LRAS truck, and I asked them what they were shooting at, and they said they were taking contact from two lights up ahead, and I asked the LRAS guys how far away those lights were. He said 1800 meters and I looked up at the guy doing the shooting and he was using a semi automatic weapon that can shoot about 600 meters and I asked the LRAS guy if he even saw anything there and he didn't. All these Marines, all up and down the line, are just shooting at nothing so that was my first interaction with the Marines, and that was a little disheartening. A lot of them didn't have any night vision equipment at all. They were shooting star clusters to see if anybody was coming up the side of the highway in front of them.[10]

SSG Jimmy Amyett, from TF 2-2, recalled, "When I took my section clearing, I had a tank with me. There were always Bradleys and tanks all along mixed in with us, so if we ran into a problem with a building, we didn't go running into the building; we ran up to the tank and had them take it out. The way I understood it and when I saw them, the Marines were just operating strictly dismounted . . . and left their armor back in support, and when they ran into trouble they would have to call it up." Like other soldiers who came in contact with the Marines in Fallujah, Amyett was convinced the Marines "could definitely have used better equipment."[11]

The second battle of Fallujah proved a costly endeavor for US forces. Although casualties were light compared to urban combat in the past, 70 Americans were killed and over 600 wounded.[12] Not surprisingly, the majority of casualties were Marines. Marine doctrine stresses the importance of using tanks as an infantry support weapon. In the battle of Fallujah, however, it may be argued they lacked enough tanks to support most of their infantry during the fierce house-to-house clearing operations. This concern was voiced by a few Army officers, many of whom felt frustrated as they watched Marines sustain heavy and perhaps avoidable casualties. "What I don't understand," CPT Chris Brooke remarked, "is why you wouldn't want to use aviation before you entered a building. I know there's a lot of pride and a lot of bravery, but it's also tactical to use all the assets you have. I don't know why they did it that way; I wasn't in their shoes."[13] MAJ John Reynolds recalled TF 2-2 sending their tanks and Bradleys to assist 1/3 Marines on 16 November. Reynolds stated that the 1/3 operations officer told him "that tanks were a scarce resource with the marines and he appreciated our support."[14]

A Marine armor officer from Company C, 2d Tank Battalion brought to light part of the problem in his AAR on Operation AL FAJR:

> Ideally, one tank company would be task organized to support one infantry battalion. Operation AL FAJR proved that we can make do with less as typical in the Marine Corps by splitting 14 tanks with two infantry battalions (six and eight). However, to achieve better shock effect and to truly weight a main effort, it would have been ideal if one tank company could be dedicated to one infantry battalion. Later, C Company Tanks [were] expected to support three infantry battalions. This is very difficult to accomplish considering the high OP-TEMPO and subsequent maintenance requirements of these tanks. A single tank company should not be expected to task organize with more than two infantry battalions . . . Furthermore, the principles of warfare of mass and fires will lessen the shock action that tanks bring to the battlefield if they are piecemealed and spread too thin.[15]

Two of the Marine breaching operations in Fallujah were problematic. The muddled attempts to place a deliberate breach across the railroad berm caused major delays in the operation. The inability of 1/3 Marines to conduct a successful breaching operation completely unhinged RCT-7's battle plan, forcing TF 2-2 to fight their way to PL Fran with its right flank exposed. It can also be argued that 1 MAR DIV never fully grasped just how fast a heavy-mechanized force could move through the city. Time after time, the Marines seemed dismayed by the speed of the Army's advance. Undoubtedly, this was one of the reasons TF 2-2 often found themselves with no Marines on their flank.

In the intelligence arena, TF 2-7 reported "lash-up" problems with the Marines. TF 2-7 cited mismatched tactics, techniques, and procedures (TTPs) and dissimilar systems for a slowdown in disbursement of intelligence between the two services.[16] Almost certainly, there were times when information and intelligence sharing was slow and cumbersome. Both TF 2-7 and TF 2-2 also experienced deconfliction problems with UAVs, which on two occasions resulted in the crash of TF 2-2's UAVs.

A perception also existed among some Army officers that in a few cases, the Marines did not want their help. On more than one occasion during the battle, offers of Army heavy-mechanized assistance were refused by the Marines. While the reasons remain unclear, these actions did not sit well with the soldiers involved. In the midst of all the success and camaraderie achieved during Operation AL FAJR, a degree of parochialism and animosity undoubtedly remains.

As with any urban fight, the battle of Fallujah was won at the squad level. In the end, however, the success of the joint operation rests on the shoulders of exceptional leaders. Natonski, Shupp, Tucker, Rainey and Newell all proved the value of superb commanders in a joint environment. Under less stellar leadership, minor problems associated with the operation could have easily spiraled out of control. "I think," Shupp commented, "there was a sense of camaraderie and reliance on each other. We had to take care of our brothers, we had to get through this, and I think that's what allowed us to have the success we had and the small number of casualties we actually had for it. Just good cross talking. The differences you might see at higher headquarters never happened at the tactical level. It really was one team, one fight."[17]

The problems encountered in Operation AL FAJR were overcome by the skills of the top commanders. However, the Army and Marines may not always have the benefit of such high caliber leadership. As the war on terrorism continues, it is certain the two branches will be involved in similar operations. It is therefore vital that the problems identified in this GWOT paper be assessed and evaluated so that solutions may be formulated.

Notes

1.   "TF 2-7 CAV: Joint Operations in Fallujah," November 2004, copy in author's possession.

2.   Ibid.

3.   CPT Peter Glass, telephone interview by author, 29 March 2006.

4.   SSG David Bellavia, telephone interview by author, 27 July 2006. Bellavia would later be nominated for the DSC for his actions in Fallujah. For his complete story see the CSI Operational Leadership Experiences website http://www-cgsc.army.mil/carl/resources/csi/csi.asp.

5.   MAJ Tim Karcher, telephone interview by author, 21 June 2004.

6.   "TF 2-2 After Action Report," copy in author's possession.

7.   LTC Pete Newell, e-mail interview by author, 1 June 2006.

8.   "TF 2-7 CAV Joint Operations in Fallujah," November 2004, copy in author's possession.

9.   CSM Timothy L. Mace, telephone interview by author, 19 April 2006.

10. CPT Chris Boggiano, interview, Operational Leadership Experiences, 20 July 2006.

11. SSG Jimmy Amyett, interview, Operational Leadership Experiences, 8 August 2006.

12. Bing West, *No True Glory* (New York: Bantam Books, 2005), 316.

13. CPT Chris Brooke, telephone interview by author, 1 May 2006.

14. MAJ John Reynolds, e-mail interview by author, 17 August 2006.

15. CPT R.J. Bodisch, "Charlie Company, 2d Tank Battalion, After Action Report, Operation AL FAJR," 8 January 2005, http://www.2ndbn5thmar.com/tisop/tirefs/charlieaar.htm, last accessed 11 August 2006.

16. "TF 2-7 CAV Joint Operations in Fallujah," November 2004, copy in author's possession.

17. COL Michael Shupp, telephone interview by author, 25 March 2006.

Bibliography

Official US Army Publications

Formica, Brigadier General Richard P. Formica. Interview by Patrecia Slayden Hollis, editor, "Part II: Joint Effects for the MNC-1 in OIF II." *Field Artillery A Joint Magazine for the US Field Artillerymen*, August 2005.

Milburn, Major A.R. "Lessons Learned: Operation Phantom Fury." Marine Corps Center for Lessons Learned. 5 January 2005.

Robertson, Dr. William Glenn. "Counterattack on the Naktong, 1950." *Leavenworth Papers*, Fort Leavenworth: Combat Studies Institute, December 1985.

Official U.S. Marine Corps Publications

MCWP 3.35.3 *Military Operations on Urbanized Terrain (MOUT)* U.S. Marine Corps, 1998.

Published Articles

Gordon, John IV and Pirnie, Bruce R. "Everybody Wanted Tanks: Heavy Forces in Operation Iraqi Freedom." *Joint Forces Quarterly*, October 2005.

Keiler, Jonathan F. "Who Won the Battle of Fallujah?" *U.S. Naval Institute Proceedings*, January 2005.

Sattler, Lieutenant General John F. and Wilson, Lieutenant Colonel Daniel H. "Operation AL FAJR: The Battle of Fallujah Part *II*." *Marine Corps Gazette*, July 2005.

Books

Ballard, John R. *Fighting For Fallujah: A New Dawn for Iraq*. Westport, CT: Praeger Security International, 2006.

Ferrel, Robert H. *The Eisenhower Diaries*. New York: W.W. Norton and Co, 1981.

Gailey, Harry A. *Howlin' Mad VS The Army: Conflict in Command, Saipan 1944*. Navato, CA: Presidio Press, 1986.

Manchester, William. *American Caesar: Douglas MacArthur 1880-1964*. Boston: Little Brown and Company, 1978.

Millett, Allan R. *Semper Fidelis The History of the United States Marine Corps: The Revised and Expanded Edition*. New York: The Free Press, 1980.

Pogue, Forrest C. *George C. Marshall: Organizer of Victory*. New York: The Viking Press, 1973.

Ricks, Thomas E. *Fiasco: The American Military Adventure in Iraq*. New York: The Penguin Press, 2006.

Sorley, Lewis. *Thunderbolt: General Creighton Abrams And The Army Of His Times*. New York: Simon & Schuster, 1992.

West, Bing. *No True Glory A Frontline Account of the Battle for Fallujah*. New York: Bantam Books, 2005.

Internet Sources

Bodisch, Captain R.J. "Charlie Company, 2nd Tank Battalion After Action Report, Operation AL FAJR." 8 January 2005. http://www.2ndbn5thmar. com/tisop/tirefs/charlieaar.htm

Cavallaro, Gina. "Old Parochialisms of U.S. Services Have Yielded to Cross-Pollination, Battlefield Commander Says." *Defense News Media Group Conferences*. http://www.defensenews.com/promos/conferences/ jw/1204577.html (accessed 1 March 2006).

O'Donnell, James P. "The Struggle For Survival." *GlobalSecurity.org*. http:// www.globalsecurity.org/military/library/report/1985/ojp.htm (accessed 1 June 2006).

Truman, Harry S letter to Congressman Gordon L. McDonough, 29 August 1950. Truman Library. Public papers of the Presidents: Harry S Truman. http://trumanlibrary.org/publicpapers/viewpapers.php?pid=864 (accessed 14 May 2006).

Wood, David. "Lack of Heavy Armor Constrains Urban Options in Iraq." *Newhouse News Service*, 27 April 2004. http://www.newhousenews.com/archive/wood042704.html (accessed 1 March 2006).

Interviews

Adgie, Lieutenant Colonel Ken. Interview by author at Fort Leavenworth, Kansas 8 March 2006.

Arraf, Jane. Interview by author, digital recording, 3 April 2006.

Batiste, Major General (Ret.) John. Interview by author, e-mail, 14 April 2006.

Bellavia, SSG David. Interview by author, digital recording, 27 July 2006.

Boggiano, Captain Chris, interview, Operational Leadership Experiences, 20 July 2006.

Brooke, Captain Chris. Interview by author, digital recording, 1 May 2006.

Cobb, Captain James. Interview by author, digital recording, 2 June 2006.

DeWitt, Major (Dr.) Lisa. Interview by author, digital recording, 23 April 2006.

Erwin, Captain Michael S. Interview by author, digital recording, 19 April 2006.

Formica, Colonel Michael. Interview by author, digital recording, 21 April 2006.

Fowler, Captain Paul A. Interview by author, e-mail, 4 April 2006.

Friel, Captain Natalie. Interview by author, e-mail, 10 March 2006.

Glass, Captain Peter, Interview by author, digital recording, 29 March 2006.

Jager, Jeff. Interview by author, digital recording, 17 May 2006.

Karcher, Major Tim. Interview by author, digital recording, 14 March 2006.

Karcher, Major Tim. Interview by author, digital recording, 21 June 2006.

Krivda, Major Erik. Interview by author at Fort Leavenworth, Kansas 6 February 2006.

Krivda, Major Erik. Interview by author, e-mail, 26 May 2006.

Kurtis, Bill. Interview by author, e-mail, 25 April 2006.

Lacour, Captain Christopher. Interview by author, digital recording, 15 May 2006.

Mace, Command Sergeant Major, Timothy L. Interview by author, digital recording, 19 April 2006.

Mayfield, Captain Kirk. Interview by author, e-mail, 9 March 2006.

McConville, Colonel James C. Interview by author, digital recording, 21 April 2006.

Natonski, Major General Richard F. Interview by author, e-mail, 8 March 2006.

Newell, Lieutenant Colonel Pete. Interview by author, e-mail, 22 March 2006.

Newell, Lieutenant Colonel Pete. Interview by author, digital recording, 23 March 2006.

Newell, Lieutenant Colonel Pete. Interview by author, e-mail, 31 May 2006.

Newell Lieutenant Colonel Pete. Interview by author, e-mail, 1 June 2006.

Newell, Lieutenant Colonel Pete. Interview by author, e-mail, 7 June 2006.

Pittard, Brigadier General, Dana. Interview by author at the Combat Studies Institute, Fort Leavenworth, Kansas 23 February 2006.

Rainey, Lieutenant Colonel James. Interview by author, digital recording, 19 April 2006.

Reynolds, Lieutenant Colonel John. Interview by author, conducted at the Combat Studies Institute, Fort Leavenworth, Kansas, 14 March 2006.

Reynolds, Lieutenant Colonel John. Interview by author, e-mail, 31 May 2006.

Reynolds, Lieutenant Colonel, John. Interview by author, e-mail, 17 August 2006.

Shupp, Colonel Michael. Interview by author, digital recording, 25 March 2006.

Tracy, Major Sean. Interview by author, Fort Leavenworth, Kansas, 15 March 2006.

Twaddell, Captain Edward III. Interview by author, digital recording, 28 February 2006.

Tyler, Captain Coley D. Interview by author, digital recording, 20 April 2006.

Urrutia, Sergeant First Class John. Interview by author at Fort Leavenworth, Kansas 14 March 2006.

Newspapers

Peterson, Scott. "US forces pour into Iraqi city," *The Christian Science Monitor*, 10 November 2004.

Scarborough, Rowan. "U.S. declares insurgency broken." *The Washington Times*, 19 November 2004.

Briefing Packet

Natonski, Major General Richard F. Slide presentation packet presented to author.

Unit History

F/4 Operation Phantom Fury History of Events. No date. Copy in author's collection.

Fowler, Captain Paul A. Memorandum for Record, Narrative of Combat Actions in Fallujah from 04 to 23 November 04. 25 November 2004. Copy in author's file.

McCrum, First Lieutenant Gregory D. *Lessons Learned: Medical Employment During the Battle for Fallujah*, no date.

Memorandum For Record, Subject: Task Force 2nd Battalion 2nd Infantry Regiment Operation Phantom Fury, 2 January 2005, copy in author's file.

Narrative Recommendation For Award Of The Silver Star To Captain Sean P. Sims, copy in author's file.

Newell, Lieutenant Colonel, Peter A. Memorandum For Record. Subject: Task Force 2nd Battalion 2nd Infantry Regiment Operation Phantom Fury. 2 January 2005. Copy in author's file.

Reynolds, Lieutenant Colonel John. Task Force 2-2 Infantry Operation Phantom Fury Summary, copy in author's file, no date.

TF 2-2 After Action Report, no date, copy in author's collection.

TF 2-7 CAV Joint Operations in Fallujah November 2004 Lessons Learned Packet produced by TF 2-7 staff.

About the Author

Matt M. Matthews joined the Combat Studies Institute in July 2005 after working for 16 years as a member of the World Class Opposing Force (OPFOR) for the Battle Command Training Program at Fort Leavenworth, Kansas. Mr. Matthews graduated from Kansas State University in 1986 with a B.S. in History. He served as an Infantry enlisted man in the Regular Army from 1977 to 1981; a Cavalry officer in the US Army Reserve from 1983 to 1986; and as an Armor officer in the Kansas Army National Guard from 1986 to 1991. Mr. Matthews recently authored *The Posse Comitatus Act and the United States Army: A Historical Perspective*. He has coauthored numerous scholarly articles on the Civil War in the Trans-Mississippi to include "Shot All To Pieces: The Battle of Lone Jack," "To Play a Bold Game: The Battle of Honey Springs," and "Better Off in Hell: The Evolution of the Kansas Red Legs"; he is a frequent speaker at Civil War Roundtables; and he recently appeared on the History Channel as a historian for Bill Kurtis' *Investigating History*. Mr. Matthews was the mayor of Ottawa, Kansas.